SHOULDER
TO
SHOULDER

Praise for *Shoulder to Shoulder*

. . . humorous . . . practical . . . insightful . . . and straight from the shoulder. Dan Reiland has been both "hoss and driver" of the wagon called the Church of Jesus Christ. He has pulled the burden as a staff member and, as executive pastor, has been the leader of the staff. And from both points of view, Dan shows you that church work is the greatest work in the world. That is why I recommend that everyone read this book.

Everyone who loves John Maxwell and appreciates the success of John's ministry at Skyline Wesleyan Church will love *Shoulder to Shoulder* and appreciate the contribution of Dan Reiland.

Elmer L. Towns
Dean, School of Religion
Liberty University

Want to be a difference-maker? The wisdom, humor, and refreshing candor of this delightful book will give you a new appreciation for your pastor. This is a win-win-win book! You will grow personally, your pastor will be encouraged by your support, and God will be blessed by the positive difference in your church.

Zig Ziglar
Chairman and Founder
Zig Ziglar Corporation

As I read through the pages of *Shoulder to Shoulder* I found myself saying *Amen* out loud, and I was all by myself! How I wish this book had been available to the laymen of the two churches I have pastored. Dan Reiland has spoken to some of the most important issues facing church leadership today! For me the message goes beyond written words! I watched from across town as Dan poured his life out in ministry to the Skyline Wesleyan Church. During days of great growth and outreach, he stood *shoulder to shoulder* with Pastor John Maxwell, and together they made a mark for God in our city. Thank God he took good notes! Now we can all learn what it really takes to make a great church . . . leaders and laymen standing *Shoulder to Shoulder*!

Dr. David Jeremiah
Senior Pastor, Shadow Mountain Community Church
President, Christian Heritage College

As I speak in many churches I am constantly discouraged at how little support the pastor gets from his people. They seem to spend more time finding what is wrong with him than lifting him up in practice and in prayer. I have observed Dan Reiland over the years and feel that his words of encouragement to the local church can be just the catalyst they are waiting for to bring harmony and progress to the church.

Florence Littauer
Author, *Personality Plus* and *Silver Boxes*

SHOULDER
TO
SHOULDER

STRENGTHENING YOUR CHURCH
BY SUPPORTING YOUR PASTOR

DAN REILAND

THOMAS NELSON PUBLISHERS
Nashville • Atlanta • London • Vancouver

Published in Nashville, Tennessee, by Thomas Nelson, Inc.

Library of Congress Cataloging-in-Publication Data
Reiland, Dan.
Shoulder to shoulder : strengthening your church by supporting your pastor / Dan Reiland.
p.   cm.
Includes bibliographical references.
ISBN 0-7852-7248-8 (pbk.)
1. Christian life. 2. Laity. 3. Clergy—Office. I. Title.
BV4520.R44 1997
253—dc21   96–39916
                                                          CIP

Printed in the United States of America.

7 8 9 10 11 12 13 14 15 QPV 04 03 02 01 00 99

It's rare in life to receive so much from one person
To receive opportunities, encouragement, and guidance
To receive love, loyalty, and lifelong lessons
And most of all, to be believed in . . .

This book is dedicated with gratitude to
My pastor, mentor, and friend
John Maxwell

Contents

FOREWORD

It is with great delight that I write this foreword for my friend Dan Reiland. The following words will reveal the love and respect I have for him.

My wife, Margaret, and I met Dan and his wife, Patti, in April 1982. He was graduating from seminary. I was interviewing him for the position of student intern for my church, Skyline Wesleyan Church, in San Diego. It was quickly obvious to both Margaret and me that Dan had great potential as a minister. What was not as apparent to us on that day was the incredible friendship that would be formed in our lives and the rewarding partnership we would together experience in ministry. Fifteen years later, we are still serving God and His people together. The reasons for this wonderful partnership are the following:

First, Dan has a teachable spirit. It has been my joy to mentor and disciple hundreds of people. No one has ever listened more intently, applied my principles more quickly, or grown so tremendously as Dan has. It has been said that we learn best from people we like most. Both of us would say "Amen" to that statement!

Second, Dan loves the local church—he eats, breathes, and sleeps it! Talk to him about pastors and his eyes light up. Suggest to him that laypeople are the keys to success of the church, and Dan leans forward and nods. Ask him a question about the local church and you'll be amazed at the insight that he shares with you. Both of us have dedicated our lives to the growth and health of the local church.

Third, Dan grows people and their ministries. In fact, he is the most fruitful staff member who has ever worked with me. Several years ago I gave him a sagging Sunday school to lead. He took it from eleven hundred to twenty-seven hundred in attendance. A few years later I asked him to develop a strong lay ministry program at our church. He grew it from 112 laity who had a weekly ministry in the church to over eighteen hundred people. After that, I asked him to start our small-group ministry at Skyline. Within two years we went from no small groups to over one hundred groups with fourteen hundred attending them on a weekly basis. What more can I say?

He became my executive pastor and led the daily operations, including leadership of the entire pastoral staff, of Skyline Wesleyan Church, with a congregation of over three thousand people in weekly attendance. He mentored more than one hundred men within the church and guaranteed the next generation a group of godly leaders. He developed one of the finest pastoral staff teams in America.

God called me to a full-time ministry to pastors; Dan felt the call as well. The night I resigned as senior pastor of Skyline, I shared with the church board that the church's greatest loss would not be me, but Dan Reiland. Today, I would still agree with this statement.

Often I have said, "We teach what we know but we reproduce what we are." Dan Reiland has raised up many laymen to walk alongside their pastor to make a positive difference within the life of the leader and the congregation.

I remember going to a lay retreat in 1988 that Dan was leading. With him were laymen whom he had developed. That day as I shared my heart with them, I could feel their support. It was as if they had been on a spiritual journey with me. At the close of our session I shared this observation with Dan. I will never forget his words to me: "John, they are with you. All my teaching has been to bond them to you, not me. You're the leader and we want to support and strengthen you!" That day I knew Dan was helping me climb to a higher level as a Christian and a pastor. I was excited!

Today I am excited for you as a pastor or a layman. Through this book, Dan is going to walk into your life and lift you to a higher level, just as he did for me.

You are about to learn many life-changing principles, insights, and practical tips. Here are just a few highlights:

1. Thought-provoking insights on the life of a pastor
2. The power of a partnership
3. The five components of a winning team
4. The blessing of speaking the truth in love
5. How to "connect" with your pastor
6. The five most important priorities in your church
7. How to pray strategically for your pastor
8. How to find your place on the ministry team
9. Living with a spirit of generosity
10. The essential role of leadership in the local church

I know you will enjoy Dan as much as I have.

John Maxwell

Note from the author. Pastors in this book are generally referred to as "he's," not to discriminate but for reading ease. The principles in this book are not limited to any gender or denomination.

– 1 –
"I THOUGHT MY PASTOR WAS SUPPOSED TO SUPPORT ME"

"'It's my pastor's job to look after my needs'—or so I believed," said church board member Bob Whitelaw. "My thinking began to change as I got more involved, and now I delight in supporting my pastor. The blessing far exceeds the investment."

Here is Bob's story:

My thinking began to change about eight years ago. My family and I visited a new church and felt immediately accepted. Through the warm welcome of the congregation and several pastors, we began to get involved in leading and ministering to people. This gave us the opportunity to be in close contact with the leadership.

I believed that the pastor's job was essentially to care for the people. I began questioning my viewpoint when I saw all the needs and problems of the congregation that went directly to the pastors. I realized for the first time that the commitment the pastors demonstrated to the people was paid with a great price: unending hours of work that is never complete. Emotional exhaustion from counseling appointment after counseling appointment. Dealing with difficult business questions where the needs exceed the resources. Direct spiritual confrontation with the enemy, who has no greater delight than seeing a pastor stumble or burn out in ministry. All this plus a family to support and raise at the same time.

My heart has now changed. God did not put the pastor

here just to preach sermons and meet my needs. God
ordained a unique partnership between my pastor and
me.

Pastors are only people. They have strengths and
weaknesses like the rest of us. While God does minister
to them through Scripture and the Holy Spirit, He has
called *me* to support my pastor as well.

Bob Whitelaw is a banking executive, father of two beautiful daughters, and a committed lay leader in the church. He
and his wife, Denise, are faithful and loyal cheerleaders of the
pastoral team in their church. They have learned firsthand the
value and blessing of supporting their pastor.

GOD HAS A PARTNERSHIP IN MIND

Bob's situation is not unique. Your pastor needs you, and
you need your pastor. God designed this unique relationship
to be a partnership. The fruit of this relationship results in
glory to God and growth in your church. God's vision and
plan for reaching the world cannot be accomplished with just
pastors and no laypeople. When Jesus launched His ministry,
even He, the Son of God, chose twelve men to help Him. Your
pastor cannot do it alone.

God s plan is for you to be an integral part in the process
of building His church. God's purpose for you is to make a
difference in this world. Like your pastor, you cannot make a
lasting impact of eternal value alone. But together, with
God's blessing, there is nothing you and your pastor cannot
accomplish. Author and playwright George Bernard Shaw
wrote these powerful words about living life to its fullest and
accomplishing great things:

This is the true joy in life—being used for a purpose recog
nized by yourself as a mighty one, being a force of nature
instead of a feverish, selfish little clod of ailments and
grievances, complaining that the world will not devote itself

to making you happy. I am of the opinion that my life belongs to the whole community as long as I live, it is my privilege to do for it whatever I can. I want to be thoroughly used up when I die, for the harder I work, the more I live. I rejoice in life for its own sake. Life is no brief candle to me. It is a sort of splendid torch which I've got a hold of for the moment, and I want to make it burn as brightly as possible before handing it on to future generations.

Those of us who carry the name *Christian* have woven into our very beings the desire to please God and live a life of significance. No Christian, in his heart of hearts, is satisfied to simply exist and wait till Jesus returns. God does not want you to live life in the random chaos of the "pinball principle," just hoping not to get bounced around too hard before being shot out again the next day only to be bounced around some more. Your destiny is not to finally slide by the swinging paddles to rest in oblivion. Take charge of the paddles! Seek God's guidance and launch yourself into life with a purpose and a passion.

ARE YOU MAXIMIZING YOUR POTENTIAL FOR GOD?

In his book *Who Switched the Price Tags?* Anthony Campolo related the words of the pastor of a Baptist church, speaking to a group of college students in his congregation:

"Children," he said, "you're going to die! . . . One of these days, they're going to take you out to the cemetery, drop you in a hole, throw some dirt on your face, and go back to the church and eat potato salad.

"When you were born," he said, "you alone were crying and everybody else was happy. The important question I want to ask is this: When you die, are you alone going to be happy, leaving everybody else crying? The answer depends on whether you live to get titles or live to get testimonies. When they lay you in the grave, are people going to stand around reciting the fancy titles you earned, or are they going to stand around giving testimonies of the good things you did for them? . . . Will you leave behind just a newspaper column telling people how important you were, or will you leave crying people who give testimonies of how they've lost the best friend they ever had?"[1]

God ordained the church as the means by which you fulfill your potential. The church is the vehicle through which a Christian can make a difference. The church is the organized *instrument* of world impact, and you are the *agent* of that impact. The pastor is God's chosen leader to guide that process. The big picture of God's plan includes both you and the pastor but is ultimately about His agenda to change people's lives with the truth of Jesus Christ.

This God-ordained partnership with your pastor is one of the most fulfilling relationships you can ever experience, because God's blessing is upon it. Your role in this relationship is vital. Your pastor is required to be many different things to many different people, which makes it difficult for him to know everyone in depth. Your desire and ability to know and understand your pastor are essential to this special partnership. This may or may not result in a personal friendship with the pastor but will greatly enable you to support your pastor and your church and to find fulfillment in God's plan for you.

DISCOVERING YOUR "REAL" VERSUS YOUR "IDEAL" PASTOR

The first step to supporting your pastor is getting to know him. How can you do this when his calendar is so full that he has to schedule time to see his family? How can you avoid being one more task on his list? Ultimately, of course, you will need a little time with him, but let me present to you several insights that will launch you light-years forward in knowing your pastor.

Seven Common Misconceptions About a Pastor's Life

I have compiled the most common misconceptions people have about their pastor based on my more than fifteen years of experience being one!

1. Pastors have an easy job.

"Other than your sermon, what do you do all week?" "Do you do this full-time?" "I would love to have a job like yours." These are statements frequently made to pastors by well-meaning Christians. They assume that a pastor's life includes some preaching, a little people-helping time, and of course, golf. This is a stereotype, not an accurate depiction of a pastor's life. Our understanding of any career we are not familiar with is very limited, whether it's that of a schoolteacher, a police officer, a carpenter, a lawyer, or a marketing director. We just don't know the realities of their day-to-day demands and responsibilities.

Recently, I took my car to the shop for an emissions test. This was a very simple and quick process that cost me about forty dollars in money and five minutes in time. The mechanic and I were talking during the test and he said, "Man, I wish I could just do these all day. This is almost as easy as you passing the plate on Sunday morning." I must confess I lost my immediate concern for his eternal salvation. For now, let's agree that he knows as little about the church as I do about cars. The difference is that I do not assume his work is easy. Don't assume the same about your pastor.

2. Pastors have a model family.

Many laypeople believe a pastor's family looks like this: When they all get up in the morning, the kids chirp like sweet little birds while the pastor's spouse plays their favorite praise songs on the piano. The pastor usually makes breakfast for the whole family while memorizing Scripture. After breakfast they settle in for an hour of prayer together and then set off on their day. When the pastor arrives home from the church office, thanks to the pastor's spouse, dinner is hot and waiting on the table. The kids are dressed immaculately and eager to share all they have learned in school. After dinner they race to do their homework and later willingly go to bed so as to be refreshed for a new day's opportunities. The pastor and his spouse read the paper, discuss world events, pray for at least one hour, and retire for the evening.

Okay, so I exaggerated a little, but the impressions I have heard over the years are not too different in concept from this fantasy description. But guess what? Our families are just like yours!

3. Pastors are experts in their field.

Because pastors invest four years in Bible college, three years in seminary, and all seven of those years talking to God, they are expected to be prepared for anything the local church throws their way. In addition, because there are no real-world business demands on pastors, they are able to concentrate completely on all the spiritual issues in the church. They need not fret about rent, politics, or the homeless.

To the contrary, every day of a pastor's ministry is filled with real-world issues, business-related and otherwise. For example, during the last nine years, our church has been involved in the process of relocating our complete facility seven miles eastward to one hundred acres of land not zoned for a church. The complications of a twenty-million-dollar project, which contain problems from environmental issues to public concern, are things a pastor is not trained for. Nevertheless, he is expected to capably handle these problems as well as the spiritual ones in his community.

4. Pastors are blessed with ideal marriages.

A pastor in a local church setting does a good amount of marriage counseling, preaches on biblical marriages, performs weddings, and on occasion, conducts weekend marriage retreats. He cares about the couples in his church and does a good job with these important responsibilities. This is often translated into the misconception that the typical pastoral couple look a lot like Ward and June Cleaver, or perhaps even Romeo and Juliet. The truth is, a pastor's marriage has to endure the same ups and downs as any other committed couple's.

5. Pastors enjoy the fellowship of many close friends.

It's easy to understand how this misconception would develop. The size of the congregation is the only limitation to the number of friends a pastor can cultivate and enjoy. If there are eighty-six people in the church, many people reason, then there is nothing preventing fifty or sixty close friendships, if not eighty-six! After all, the pastor spends all his time with these people! Imagine a pastor with five hundred people in his church—there would be unbelievable opportunity for friendships to blossom. Even if they were not all close relationships, certainly he would have far more friends than the average person.

In reality, many would be surprised to learn how few people a pastor can really call "friend."

6. Pastors consistently experience a vibrant walk with God.

This is the most common in the list of misconceptions. Members of the church often make the assumption that the pastor invests large portions of his day in Bible study, prayer, meditation, Scripture memorization, and personal worship While your pastor is certainly well acquainted with these areas, it may surprise you to know how little time he is able to give to each of these areas—not because of a lack of desire, but because of a lack of time.

I remember a phone call from a church member having marriage troubles. The phone call came at 11:00 P.M., and the caller requested that I come to his home on a regular basis to give him and his wife counsel. This is only one example of hundreds, and when added up, the total amount of time is staggering. Because pastors genuinely desire to help, and the congregation expects the help, there is little time left for the "quiet disciplines."

7. Pastors are content and fulfilled in their work.

The following are actual statements received by pastors: "It must be great to not have to mess with the 'worldly' things of the day-to-day business world, to be able to focus only on God and good Christian people." "Isn't it great that your house (parsonage) is right next to the church?" "It must be wonderful to always be doing exactly what God wants you to do."

When I hear statements like these, I smile and acknowledge the blessing of ministry, but I also realize the strength of the misconception. The assumption of contentment and fulfillment often comes from the connection of church and spiritual life, as well as the pastor's own personal call to ministry.

This list of misperceptions is not comprehensive, but it covers the big picture of traditional thinking when it comes to the life and ministry of a local church pastor. The next list is the corresponding response to each of the misconceptions.

Seven Common Realities of a Pastor's Life

The following seven "realities" are obviously not all true at the same time for any one pastor. But nearly all pastors experience many of these over the course of their ministry.

1. Pastors have a challenging and demanding job.

God teaches us in Ephesians 4:12 that the pastor's primary role is to equip the *people in the church* to do the ministry. That's right! The pastor is the recruiter, motivator, and equipper, and the people are the real ministers. The pastor is the coach and the people are the players. The opposite usually takes place in most churches, where the pastor does nearly everything, or attempts to. The truth is he can't. Your pastor needs you, and so does God, to build the church.

Think of the church as a make-believe hospital where your

doctor is available twenty-four hours a day, specializes in all areas, and charges no fees. If you like what he does, you may come back with something else for him to "fix" and maybe drop a little something in the "plate." And no matter what, the doctor is happy to see you! Sound impossible? You're right!

The point is not that the pastor's job is more difficult than anyone else's, but it is at least as challenging and demanding as other professions. A 1991 survey of pastors conducted by Fuller Church Growth Institute revealed that 90 percent of pastors work more than forty-six hours a week.[2] As I talk with pastors across America, more than half reveal they work more than sixty hours a week.

The vast majority of all churches in America have less than two hundred people in attendance on a Sunday morning. The official job description contains these five basic areas: preacher, evangelist, counselor, hospital and home visitor, and wedding and funeral officiator. While these are all valid responsibilities of ministry in the local church, they do not follow the pastor's biblical purpose and priorities mentioned earlier.

The pastor's unofficial, but very real job description looks like this:

1. Motivator
2. Song leader
3. Youth guidance counselor
4. Foreign missions expert
5. Field trip organizer
6. Social worker
7. Hospital chaplain
8. Prison ministry representative
9. Marketing director
10. Fund-raiser
11. Legal representative

12. Accountant
13. Building repair specialist
14. Diplomat
15. Negotiator
16. Purchasing agent
17. Arbitrator
18. Soccer coach
19. Marriage, family, and child counselor
20. Orator
21. Entertainer
22. Biblical scholar
23. Chief operations officer
24. Teacher
25. Emergency plumber

This list is not comprehensive, but I'm sure you get the point.

The pastor is God's servant, but he is viewed as a "public servant." The expectations of the congregation are often unrealistic, even in larger churches where large staffs allow pastors to focus on fewer and more specialized areas. However, in the larger churches the more focused job description is complicated by a much larger number of people under the umbrella of a pastor's responsibility.

One of the more subtle but substantial challenges of the pastor's job is this: While most reasonable people would look at this list and quickly agree that it is not realistic, those same people in their moment of need will make an exception for whatever point of service they desire. In other words, people in need rarely stop to consider a pastor's real job description. And the typical pastor is not a complainer but a hardworking, God-fearing servant, so he usually jumps right in to meet the need. The demands of ministry do not allow the pastor to focus on priorities. The people can end up feeling frustrated because the pastor can only partially meet needs that he is neither trained, nor has sufficient time, to accomplish.

2. Pastors have a stressful family life.

The Fuller Church Growth Institute survey reports that 80 percent of pastors believe that ministry has negatively affected their families. The same survey reports that 33 percent of pastors say that being in the ministry is an outright hazard to their family.[3]

What would cause such findings? The number-one issue is the massive demand on a pastor's time and the twenty-four-hour "on call" nature of the work. The pastor himself can usually handle the pressure, and often the pastor's spouse can as well, but the children are the ones who suffer. They are not equipped to understand or cope with the normal pressures and challenges of the pastoral home.

A second issue is the emotional drain of pastoral ministry. In one ten-hour day a pastor can easily work with a divorce situation, a teenage pregnancy, an unhappy board member, a financial crisis, a staff discipline issue, and the youth bus breaking down in the mountains with twenty-seven of his congregation's teenagers on board. (The teens love it, but parents are not happy, and it is now the pastor's job to fix the bus and get the kids home!) After a day like this, the Sunday sermon is a long way from complete, and there isn't much energy left for the family.

Another factor is the Fishbowl Syndrome. There is a certain expectation for the pastor's family to be as flawless as possible. The congregation is always watching what the pastor's family is doing. It's an unspoken credibility thermometer to which the members of the church all have access. The pastor and his family desire to be good role models for the congregation, so they constantly strive to live a model life. The stress of the attempt often results in more family conflict rather than the ideal example.

You might be thinking, *Hey, isn't the pastor's family the pastor's responsibility? Don't blame the condition of the pastor's family on me.* Yes, ultimately his family is his responsibility, and no blame is intended here. The point is to sensitize the church to the situation and encourage you to be an advocate of your pastor's time at home with his family. You can be as much an encourager of the pastor's family life as he is of yours. This is the God-ordained partnership in action.

3. Pastors often feel inadequate in their work.

When you consider the job descriptions that have been listed, it is a natural result for any honest pastor to feel less than fully qualified for the job. The Fuller survey reports that 50 percent of pastors feel unable to meet the needs of the job and 90 percent feel they were inadequately trained to cope with ministry demands.[4]

Seminary does an excellent job of preparing pastors in the biblical and theological arenas of pastoral ministry. Seminaries do not, however, specialize in the practical areas of leadership training for the pastor—mobilizing volunteers, attitude development, and general people skills. These are foundational essentials necessary for him to be successful in local church ministry.

4. Pastors experience tension in their marriages.

This doesn't mean that the typical pastoral couple are in trouble. It means they are human and face the same kinds of life pressures that other couples do. The difference is that the pastoral couple often have no one in the church who serves as confidant and encourager. Part of the responsibility certainly rests upon the pastor's willingness to risk authenticity in this area. But the truth is that the average congregation is more interested in the pastor meeting their needs than they are stepping into the ministry partnership and getting to know their "real" pastor. This is not a critical statement about the average congregation; it is written with the understanding of the typical member's viewpoint of the pastor's job description. They are neither selfish nor imposing if they believe the pastor's job description is to meet many of their personal needs. It is—but he has needs too.

The stresses listed in Reality #2—time demands, emotional

pressures, and the Fishbowl Syndrome—have an equally significant impact on the pastoral marriage. Tragically, there is an alarming number of moral failures among clergy marriages. The adultery and divorce rates of clergy couples are less than that of nonclergy Christian couples, but even one is too many. Pastors and their wives are subject to a higher degree of temptation than other Christian couples. Satan knows that if he can cause them to stumble and fall, he can hurt, if not destroy, an entire congregation at the same time. Even if Satan cannot orchestrate a complete marriage failure, the distraction that results from tension in the relationship causes the pastor to be less effective in his ministry.

5. Pastors suffer from loneliness.

Several years ago at a lunch with John Maxwell and Fred Smith, Sr. (a successful Christian businessman in Texas, who has the spiritual gift of wisdom), I had the opportunity to ask two outstanding leaders any question I desired. Not being prepared, I fired a shotgun question to see what I would learn. I asked, "What is the one universal experience that a leader in any arena (church, business, etc.) will encounter?" Their response was amazing, almost as if it was rehearsed. In perfect simulcast stereo, they said, "Loneliness." This idea is often a great surprise to members of a congregation. "How could our pastor possibly be lonely, when he is with people all the time?" It's a different kind of loneliness. It's a leadership loneliness, one that comes with the territory. It is quite possible to be with people all day long and still feel alone.

The Fuller survey findings report that 70 percent of pastors do not have someone they consider a close friend.[5] This is an incredibly large percentage of pastors who do not share a close relationship with someone outside their marriage. There are at least five reasons for leadership loneliness:

- **Reason 1: Leadership loneliness comes from the responsibility of making difficult decisions.**

- Reason 2: Leadership loneliness is experienced by the pastor because of his commitment to confidentiality.
- Reason 3: Leadership loneliness is caused by pastors themselves who are unwilling to be known for their true selves, as a result of attempting to live up to years of role expectations.
- Reason 4: Leadership loneliness comes from the weight or "load" of leadership itself.
- Reason 5: Leadership loneliness is experienced from the spiritual disciplines of study and prayer.

Pastors are willing to accept this "lonely" aspect of their calling, but having a better awareness of this reality will enable you to be a great encourager to your pastor. Let him know that you are in the game with him, and together you can build the church in a way that glorifies God and truly meets people's needs.

6. Pastors go through spiritually dry seasons.

Every pastor faces the danger of his call becoming his career. When a pastor is immersed in "spiritual" issues, what was once alive in his heart can become merely business in his head. The pastor hasn't stopped loving God or lost his call to ministry. He certainly doesn't care any less for the people. He simply has allowed what was once the fire and passion of his soul to become the routine of his work.

If the pastor is running in high gear for long periods of time without replenishing himself through personal quiet times, his spiritual reservoir will run dry. The pastor, his family, and eventually the entire congregation will suffer from this spiritually dry season. The longer the season, the greater the impact.

Pastors are also subject to a greater level of spiritual warfare. Simply put, Satan realizes that if he can successfully attack the pastor he can cause damage to the entire congregation. Satan attacks the pastor in the same ways he attacks you. He uses tactics such as discouragement, worldly temptations, and complacency, but targets the pastor with a much greater intensity. Pastors are particularly vulnerable during spiritually dry seasons.

I use the word *season* carefully and intentionally. Seasons pass in time but also return. If the pastor has grown and strengthened himself, when the next dry season hits he is better prepared and weathers it well. Long, cold winters give way to beautiful springtime newness, but only with a closeness and dependence upon God. You can play a critical role in God's kingdom by encouraging your pastor and praying that his heart stays hot for God.

7. Pastors are well acquainted with discouragement.

There are numerous causes of discouragement in a pastor's life:

- **Discouragement is caused by conflict with people.**
- **Discouragement is caused by lack of commitment from people.**
- **Discouragement comes from personal attacks from people.**

Pastor Paul (the apostle) was well acquainted with hardship and discouragement. That is why Barnabas and Timothy meant so much to him. Barney and Tim were his loyal supporters and partners in ministry. When Paul was near his date of execution, he called for Timothy. He wanted the support of those closest to him. As you read 2 Timothy 4:9–18 you can feel Paul's passion as he expresses gratitude for the support of his friends, yet discouragement from the opposition and loneliness he is facing.

> Do your best to come to me quickly, for Demas, because he loved this world, has *deserted me* and has gone to Thessalonica. Crescens has gone to Galatia, and Titus to Dalmatia. *Only Luke is with me. Get Mark and bring him with you,* because he is helpful to me in my ministry. I sent Tychicus

to Ephesus. When you come, bring the cloak that I left with
Carpus at Troas, and my scrolls, especially the parchments.

Alexander the metalworker did me a great deal of harm. The
Lord will repay him for what he has done. You too should be
on your guard against him, because *he strongly opposed our
message.*

*At my first defense, no one came to my support, but everyone
deserted me.* May it not be held against them. *But the Lord
stood at my side* and gave me strength, so that through me
the message might be fully proclaimed and all the Gentiles
might hear it. And I was delivered from the lion's mouth.
The Lord will rescue me from every evil attack and will
bring me safely to his heavenly kingdom. To him be glory
for ever and ever. (italics mine)

Yes, the Lord rescued Paul and spiritually encouraged him.
But the fact remains that there is a deep human need to be
supported by other human beings. Pastors haven't changed
since Paul's time. If anything, times are much more complicated and the need for support is even greater. You can make
a substantial difference in God's kingdom by helping your
pastor build your church.

SUPPORT IS GOD'S IDEA

One of my favorite Old Testament stories is about Moses
and the Israelites in battle with the Amalekites. As long as
Moses held up his hands they won, but when Moses lowered
his arms from fatigue, they got whipped. Enjoy this great
story found in Exodus 17:8–13.

Now Amalek came and fought with Israel in Rephidim. And
Moses said to Joshua, "Choose us some men and go out,
fight with Amalek. Tomorrow I will stand on the top of the
hill with the rod of God in my hand."

So Joshua did as Moses said to him, and fought with
Amalek. And Moses, Aaron, and Hur went up to the top of

the hill. And so it was, when Moses held up his hand, that Israel prevailed; and when he let down his hand, Amalek prevailed. *But Moses' hands became heavy;* so they took a stone and put it under him, and he sat on it. *And Aaron and Hur supported his hands,* one on one side, and the other on the other side; and his hands were steady until the going down of the sun. So Joshua defeated Amalek and his people with the edge of the sword. (NKJV; italics mine)

God gave us a beautiful picture of support. Will you lift the arms of your pastor? He truly needs your help. When you do so, God is pleased with the spirit of unity and teamwork, the pastor is encouraged, and your church realizes growth.

FEW ARE CALLED TO LEAD, MANY ARE NEEDED TO SUPPORT

When I was a young boy, when there were too many people in the kitchen and they all wanted to give direction, my mom had a favorite saying: "Too many chiefs and not enough Indians!" That was our clue that it was time to scram before the big chief scalped some of her own braves.

The nature of leadership declares that fewer leaders are needed than faithful people who will support the leader in his vision. This is a simple point of logic. The pastor is the leader. While there are other leaders in the church who are vital to the ministry team, there is only one who casts the vision and carries the responsibility of the bottom line. As in my mother's kitchen, there is room for only one chief. However, there is a great deal of work to be done in other rooms throughout the house. There is literally no limit to the amount of aid and ability needed in the rooms of God's house.

I don't want to oversimplify the point by calling it a "numbers issue," but the numbers matter. There is one pastor and dozens, scores, or even hundreds of others in the church. The pastor could not possibly support all these people, but this same congregation could rise up like a mighty army for God and support the pastor in the work of building the church. There is virtually nothing that could not be accomplished for the glory of God with this unity of spirit and commitment. Ultimately, your support is the essential ingredient for a successful partnership with your pastor.

A PERSONAL TOUCH

As this first chapter comes to a close, let me share a perspective from the other side of the desk—my pastor's heart. I have a unique vantage point in writing to you about supporting your pastor. For more than thirteen years I have found great joy, blessing, and personal fulfillment in supporting my pastor, John Maxwell. During those same years, I deeply appreciated the support given to me from laymen who understood the need to come alongside their pastor and "lift his arms" in the battle.

It all started with a lesson on leadership. "Everything rises and falls on leadership." The words of John Maxwell, the new senior pastor at Skyline Wesleyan Church in San Diego, California, struck a chord of truth in my heart and mind. He was bold, confident, and enthusiastic. I liked him immediately. I knew I could follow him, and even more important, he could lead me on a journey that would encourage both kingdom and personal growth. Neither my wife, Patti, nor I had any idea what was in store.

"The pastor is the leader and equipper and the people are the ministers," John taught from Ephesians 4:11–12. "Partners in ministry" was a biblical theme, but new to me. Not only was it impossible for the pastor to do it all, God didn't design it that way. Every pastor needed to have a core of supporters around him. John talked about the encouragement of his father and the prayers of his mother. He spoke of the cheerful, intentional, and totally committed support of his wife, Margaret. John talked about the entire congregation partnering in ministry and supporting God's call on his life to lead their church in a way that would be pleasing to God.

I knew this was it. It was the direction I needed. I was so fascinated by the way this information would reshape my ministry, I almost forgot that Patti and I were there to interview with John Maxwell about joining his pastoral staff team upon my graduation from seminary. I was so nervous at the interview dinner that Patti finally asked Margaret in the ladies' rest room, "Well, is Dan hired or not?" Margaret replied, "Of course." They both returned to the table and informed John and me that I was on staff. (That's how John and I ran the church for the next thirteen years We still get nervous every time they go into a rest room.)

Patti and I kneeled before the Lord and John prayed an anointed prayer over us. Tears ran down our faces. We felt supported and knew someone believed in us. We went back to the hotel room that evening and knelt down by the bed. We wrote a letter to God of commitment to a soul-winning and life-changing ministry. We knew then and still do today that it could not be accomplished alone.

During the last seven years of our ministry at Skyline Wesleyan Church, I served John and the church as the executive pastor. My responsibility was the day-to-day ministry of the church, and my joy was supporting John as the senior pastor.

It is with that experience that I write this book. The joy of supporting a pastor called and anointed of God, and the vision of knowing the ultimate impact on the kingdom of God, compels me to share this with you. I write from the unique perspective of one who supports his pastor, and also as a pastor who deeply understands the need to be supported.

Your pastor may not yet have a person to support and believe in him, but you can be that person. *I trust that through the pages of this book God will enlarge your heart for your pastor and strengthen your vision for ministry.*

───STEPS TOWARD ACTION───

1. Remember that God designed the unique ministry partnership between you and your pastor.
2. Be a good steward of your potential by tapping into God's instrument of human potential: the church.
3. Pray about how God wants you to make a difference in people's lives.
4. Remember, God is pleased when you support the "chosen" leaders of His church.
5. Think through which of the seven common misconceptions you thought were true about your pastor.
6. Think through which of the seven common "realities" may apply to your pastor.
7. Remember, few are called to lead, but many are needed to support.
8 Make a commitment to support your pastor.

- 2 -

CHAMPION YOUR PASTOR'S HUMANITY

"I always thought pastors were somehow different from the rest of us," admitted Glenn Finch. "But I have discovered that pastors are just people! Now it is my joy and blessing to encourage my pastor to simply be himself."

Here is Glenn's story:

Throughout my church life I viewed pastors as being different from "normal" people. The congregation seemed to hold them to higher, almost superhuman, standards. These expectations often led to people placing the pastor on a pedestal. The pastor then tried to be perfect in order to live up to his position on the pedestal.

It wasn't until God blessed me with a pastor as one of my closest friends that I realized these unrealistic expectations create enormous pressure. Unrealistic standards also deny pastors the ability to be themselves. And they contribute to the unhealthy idea that pastors must be everything to everyone.

As I came alongside my pastor and encouraged him to be himself and to balance his life physically, emotionally, spiritually, and with his family, I was surprised at his response. He hungered for the opportunity to be authentic. He had a great desire to share who he really was and how he really felt with a trusted friend.

Today it is a joy and a privilege to not only assist my pastor in embracing and celebrating his own humanity, but also to encourage him to simply be the person that God intended him to be—nothing more and nothing less.

Glenn Finch is a Christian attorney with two precious daughters and a wonderful wife named Lisa. They are both dedicated to serving God in their local church. Glenn is truly an advocate for pastors being themselves and invests deeply in pastors' lives as God directs him. People like Glenn can make the difference between success and failure for pastors.

THE SPACE BETWEEN SUCCESS AND FAILURE IS SMALL

The space between success and failure is as small as four letters: *r-i-s-k*. Without it, there is no success. With it, everything is on the line. Risks are taken every day: a businessman in the stock market—buy or sell? A quarterback, fourth down on the twenty-yard line—kick or go for it? A mom and kids in a minivan attempting to merge onto the freeway—hit the gas or hit the brakes? In each scenario, one choice brings victory, the other defeat.

Every pastor wants to be successful. Some of this desire comes from God's Spirit and some from the pastor's human side; both are legitimate. Since God's part is sovereignly taken care of, our focus is the human side. The place we must begin with is our recognition of our pastors' humanity and our willingness to accept and embrace it.

Risks must be taken for the church to grow. In your pastor's attempts to grow the church he will make mistakes. The bigger the church, the bigger the impact of the mistakes. But all pastors make them. The best pastors make them regularly and admit them freely. The key is in not making the same mistake over and over again. If a pastor isn't making many mistakes, he's not taking enough risks. You can support your pastor by encouraging him to make a few mistakes this month! Laugh about them, and learn from them together. Pastors tend to report successes quicker than failures, but you can make a difference by letting your pastor know you realize he is human.

One of our best flops at Skyline was our first attempt to establish a small-group ministry. The Skyline congregation is so positive and supportive that they would let us try anything—well, nearly anything—and we did. Small-group ministry wasn't so dangerous; thousands of churches across the country were giving it a go. This was in 1984 and I thought 1985 would never come. We were no more prepared to launch what we then called Care Circles than we were to launch the Space Shuttle. Actually, I now think we could have gotten the Shuttle farther off the ground!

Later, after the dust settled, the congregation affectionately referred to the "Who Cares Circles." We made so many mistakes. We tried to force a unified curriculum, which didn't work. We tried to organize the people into care groups by geographic location instead of letting people go where they desired. Most significantly, our leaders simply were not ready. But we got back up, dusted off our knees, nursed our wounds, and kept on going. We had a congregation who supported the pastors. They laughed with us and we all learned together how not to start small groups. As a result of that, several years later Home Groups were launched, grew quickly, and are still thriving today.

How about your pastor? Is he one of those human types? Do you recognize and embrace his humanity? Tell him this week that mistakes are okay, failure isn't final, and that you believe in him. This attitude is a foundational principle for success in any arena, including the church. It creates an inner freedom that fosters both dreaming big and moving forward with confidence.

GIVE YOUR PASTOR PERMISSION TO BE HIMSELF

My wife, Patti, and I were enjoying ourselves at a Christmas party hosted by her employer. Patti introduced me to several people and it soon came up in conversation that I was a pastor. One person looked at me and in all sincerity said, "You don't look like a pastor."

While it's true I bear no resemblance to Billy Graham or the Pope, the first thought that went through my mind was, *Just what does a pastor look like anyway?* Perhaps if I wore a clerical collar, or an old, worn, double-knit polyester suit, or carried a Bible so big I needed a wheelbarrow to move it around, I would look more like a pastor. I smiled, as all pastors do who have read Dale Carnegie's book on how to get along with strange people, and prayed a special prayer of blessing over him. A silent prayer.

Most pastors need permission to be themselves. You may think that ultimately this "permission" must come from inside each individual pastor. That's true, but don't forget your part in acknowledging your pastor's humanity. Most pastors need your permission because of the Fishbowl Syndrome. Feeling watched all the time can lead to great insecurity. This causes some pastors to be less than completely genuine. This is not a character flaw on their part, nor a desire to be dishonest. But imagine for a moment how you and your family would fare under such constant observation. I'm confident you would at least be cautious at times about what you say and do. I do not believe you would exercise circumspection because you were in some way hypocritical, but because of a perceived expectation that you must live a life of superhuman standards in order to be a godly role model to your congregation.

The following story is a classic example of stereotyped perceptions of a pastor. A couple of years ago I was in a local Blockbuster store to rent a video for a family video night. One person from my church approached me and said, "I didn't know *you guys* rented videos."

I didn't know exactly what to say, but once again I mustered up one of those Carnegie smiles and silently prayed a "special" prayer of blessing over him. I responded out loud by saying, "Well, of course we do. But only *Jesus of Nazareth,*

The Ten Commandments, and if we're in a really racy mood, *Ben Hur."*

The Bible says that God did forgive me for saying that, and for craftily holding the video I was renting slightly behind my back. It's not that I was actually hiding it from him, I was just having fun seeing how far he could extend his neck to try and read the title. (It was probably something like *Rambo vs. Wyatt Earp.* I love a good shoot-'em-up movie.)

Author and former pastor Chuck Swindoll rides Harley Davidson motorcycles. He was featured in *Christianity Today,* in an advertisement by his publisher, dressed in black leather from head to toe, sitting on a black Harley, with the caption overhead: *Sermonator.* It was great! How about you—would you give your pastor permission to ride a Harley to church on Sunday morning? Okay, maybe he's not the Harley type. How about a moped? The point is, will you let him be himself?

Several of my Christian buddies love to hunt and when we get together at church events they tell stories and we all have a great time. I love how the animals get larger, meaner, and farther away every time the stories are told! One summer, John Maxwell, while still senior pastor of Skyline Wesleyan Church, went on a safari with his son Joel. They bagged the big game and the stories were great. In our boyish enthusiasm we overlooked the reaction of many in the congregation. In California hunting isn't exactly the most revered sport, especially for a "man of the cloth." "Save the whales" is more likely to get a sympathetic ear. After church, one upset member cried out, *"Pastor shot Bambi!"*

"No, he really didn't," we said, but it was too late. The great white hunter was now the hunted. I asked one lady who was particularly upset if she had ever eaten hamburger, venison, lamb chops, or rabbit stew. Somehow that was "different."

Let your pastor live a little, let him be himself.

ENCOURAGE AUTHENTICITY BY BEING AUTHENTIC

"Nice sermon, Pastor." Have you ever said something like this to your pastor after he preached a sermon that wouldn't motivate you to get out of the way of an oncoming train? This exact phrase and many similar to it have been spoken thousands of times on Sunday mornings in churches across America. They are kindhearted words spoken by kindhearted people, but they're not completely honest. Both you and the pastor know the real truth about the morning's message.

I'm certainly not recommending a critical spirit that blasts the pastor at every turn. One pastor tells the story of a person in his church who bought a tape of his Sunday morning message every week. This person took it home, had it transcribed, marked every grammatical error in red, and mailed it in to the church. This is certainly an extreme, but it's a great example of how not to support your pastor.

The point is, honesty begets honesty. Openness fosters authenticity, which in turn develops mutual trust and respect. As for the example of a Sunday morning sermon, no pastor, no matter how good a communicator he is, preaches an award-winner every Sunday. He can't do this any more than the best baseball players can hit a home run every time at bat.

The first key is to communicate honestly. When your pastor gets on base, let him know. When he hits a home run, really let him know.

The second key is to communicate specifically. A good way to be specific is to tell your pastor about how your life was personally impacted or changed by the sermon. This may require that your comments follow the sermon by a few weeks. Specific, honest, from-the-heart comments have deep meaning and value to your pastor. Good comments also let him know that he is hitting the target with his preaching.

THE PASTOR HAT

People often want their pastor to take his "pastor hat" off and just be a real person like the rest of the congregation. There are two important things to know about this. First, he *is* a real person. And second, he is *not* just like the rest of the congregation. Understanding how those two factors fit together will help you support your pastor with greater impact. The pastor's primary difference from the laity comes as a result of his responsibilities as leader of the congregation. The very fact that he is the leader demands that he cannot be one of the pack. But he can be himself and enjoy meaningful relationships with you and others in the congregation.

This takes us back to a previous question. Will you allow him to be himself? Second, and equally important, will you give him the room he needs to be the leader? You can do this by not making extra demands on his time. Support his decisions, and be open and honest in your communication with him. When the pastor knows that you are authentic in what you say and do, he can respond with more freedom and intimacy. This is not to suggest that your pastor is holding back. Nor is it suggesting that he isn't willing to take the leadership position of initiative in openness and honesty. This idea finds its greatest value in your ability and your willingness to be genuine with your pastor.

GETTING READY FOR CHURCH

Getting ready for church on Sunday mornings can be chaotic. It can be nearly impossible if you have young children. The alarm fails to go off. Everyone oversleeps. Dad cuts himself as he shaves too quickly. Mom burns the breakfast as she rushes around the kitchen with only half her makeup and hair done. The kids are finally ready and one throws up on her dress, the other tears his pants as he fights with the neighbor boy. Everyone is finally in the car and it won't start. "Someone" left the lights on all night and the battery is dead, which causes an argument between Mom and Dad. You get a ride from a friend, and now you are all really late. When the pastor greets you with a cheery "Good morning, how are you?" and you respond with "Great, Pastor! Couldn't be better!" the very gates of heaven are twitching with your response.

Don't expect your pastor to be authentic with you if you are not authentic with him. Next time, say to him, "Pastor, we've had a terrible morning, but we are glad to be here." He'll find your response delightful and refreshing.

ALLOW YOUR PASTOR TO PLAY TO HIS STRENGTHS

Do you know your pastor's strengths? This is essential to be an effective supporter and part of your church's success. Pastor David Seamands did primarily two things in his large United Methodist Church in Wilmore, Kentucky. He developed and delivered outstanding biblical sermons and counseled with godly wisdom. That's it, and he did them both extremely well. The congregation knew his strengths and not only gave him permission to be himself, but set him free to do what he did best. Dr. Seamands built a great ministry by doing what he was good at.

John Maxwell's primary strengths were leadership and preaching. If he had focused on counseling as David Seamands did, Skyline church might not be in existence today. Counseling is just not John's gift! Before you get halfway through your problem he has a yellow legal pad out with a list of seventeen things you need to do to "fix" yourself. But the wise Skyline people released John from the vast majority of counseling to free him up to play to his strengths.

Learning more about your pastor's ministry style and giftedness will better enable you to allow him to play to his strengths. This is a logical process. You can encourage him toward his strengths only if you know what they are.

To discern these, there are three primary factors you need

to know. First, your pastor's leadership style; second, his personality type; and third, your pastor's spiritual gifts.

1. Your Pastor's Leadership Style

We'll begin with his preferred or natural leadership style. There are three basic leadership style preferences:

A charismatic leadership style.

This is the pastor who has an attractive personality with a pied-piper effect on his followers. People just want to be around him and are not always sure why—they just do. People follow this type of leader as naturally as the sun rises in the morning. Pastors with a charismatic leadership style can be either playful or forceful in their approach, and sometimes a little of each.

An organizational leadership style.

This is the pastor with an administrative flair who has a natural ability to see unorganized things in an organized way. This doesn't necessarily mean he is a neat freak, but it does mean he has a preference for order as opposed to chaos. Both the charismatic leader and the relational leader (to be discussed) have a greater ability to "go with the flow" and not be too concerned about organizational structure.

A relational leadership style.

This is the pastor who is absolutely great with people. There just isn't anyone he can't get along with and who doesn't seem to like him in return. This pastor's relationship skills come naturally and are highly developed. He would rather be with people than do just about anything else.

None of these three styles of leadership is better than another, and many pastors have a mixture of styles. But nearly all pastors are predominantly one of the three. Do you know the leadership style of your pastor? Here are two examples of how this will help you support your pastor and thereby help grow your church: If you try to force a nonorganizational charismatic leader into an administrative style, he will be like a fish out of water and eventually suffocate. Let him lead by casting vision and let someone else do the organizing. If you require a skilled organizational leader to invest a large portion of his time in hospital visitation and pastoral care, he will be frustrated and much less effective. Let him organize other people in the church to go out on visitation and minister in the pastoral care area.

2. Your Pastor's Personality Type

Detailed explanation of personality characteristics is not needed as there are so many excellent books on the topic. But a brief review will be helpful in the application of knowing your pastor's personality type. The four basic temperaments and their dominant characteristics are: Choleric (controlling), Sanguine (fun), Melancholy (perfectionistic), and Phlegmatic (peaceful). While these are grand generalizations, they do describe in one word the primary characteristic of each temperament and offer insight. The Choleric values speed, the bottom line, and loyalty. The Sanguine values creativity, humor, and flexibility. The Melancholy values depth, integrity, and process. The Phlegmatic values relationship, unity, and a sense of team.

Your pastor is probably a mixture of two personality types but reveals one dominant one. No type is better than another, and all four are represented in great leaders throughout history. I believe that Jesus had the strengths of all four types and the weaknesses of none.

That brings us to the application: Let your pastor play to his strength. Don't expect a sanguine pastor to catch a minute detail in a financial report. Actually, I've met some sanguine pastors who would be lucky just to find the report! Don't expect a melancholy pastor to be the life of the party, just be happy if he shows up and smiles. You get the idea, I'm sure.

3. Your Pastor's Spiritual Gifts

Depending on which gifts survey you study there are between seven and twenty-five spiritual gifts. Don't be alarmed—pastors are not just making them up as they go. The biblical references give us some latitude in the configuration of the list. The important issue is that they are recognized, developed, and used to build the body of Christ. (We will discuss spiritual gifts in more detail in Chapter 8.)

In talking with hundreds of pastors I have compiled a list of the ten most common spiritual gifts found in pastors. They are (alphabetically):

1. Administration
2. Evangelism
3. Faith
4. Intercession
5. Knowledge
6. Leadership
7. Mercy
8. Pastor/Teacher
9. Teaching
10. Wisdom

If you are not sure of your pastor's spiritual gifts, ask him about them soon. As you connect leadership style, personality type, and spiritual gifts, your pastor's strengths will become clear. Bless his strengths, and pray for God to send people who will support his weaknesses.

BE AN ADVOCATE OF REALISTIC EXPECTATIONS

The funny thing about expectations is that everyone has his own. The following is a humorous, wish-list description of "The Perfect Pastor" in the corporate eyes of a congregation. Descriptions like this have been floating around the church for years!

After hundreds of years of study and research, a model pastor has been found to suit everyone. He preaches exactly twenty minutes, and follows it with an invitation in which everyone is convicted but no one is offended. He works from 7:00 A.M. to 10:00 P.M. in every type of work from counseling to custodial service. He is twenty-seven years old and has been preaching for thirty years.

He is tall and short, thin and heavy set, handsome but not overpowering. He has one brown eye and one blue eye. His hair is parted in the middle. The left side is dark and straight. The right side is brown and wavy with a balding spot on the top revealing his maturity.

He has a burning desire to work with teenagers and spends all of his time with the older folks. He smiles constantly with a straight and sober face because he has a sense of humor that keeps him seriously at his work.

He invests twenty-five hours a week in sermon preparation, twenty hours in counseling, ten hours in meetings, five hours in emergencies, twenty hours in visitations and evangelism, six hours in weddings and funerals, thirty hours in prayer and meditation, twelve hours in letter writing and administration, and ten hours in creative thinking. He spends five evenings at home with his family, plus a day off, and always stops for interruptions.

He's a seminary graduate, but uses only one- and two-syllable words. He makes fifteen calls a day, spends all his time evangelizing the unchurched, attends all retreats, goes to all youth events, and is always available in his office. His kids are perfect, his mother is rich, and his wife plays the piano. His house is large, bank account small, and his car is in the shop. He's paid too much, too little, and he gives it all away. He's talented, gifted, scholarly, practical, popular, compassionate, understanding, patient, levelheaded, dependable, loving, caring, neat, organized, cheerful, and above all, humble.

You may be thinking, *I don't expect all that of my pastor.* I'm confident you don't, but if there are more than seventy-five people in your church, everyone's individual expectations add up to these and more!

The description of "The Perfect Pastor" is a great illustration of the expectation problem. In business, expectations are more manageable because they are more specific. If you went to a clothing store you wouldn't be upset if they didn't have power tools to sell you. You weren't expecting to find any there. If you go to a McDonald's for a hamburger you wouldn't be annoyed to find there was no Chinese food to eat. But in the church the expectations are limited only to people's imaginations.

As a father of young children there are times when I have trouble keeping up with the expectations of just two little ones. Wrestling for thirty minutes is one thing, but wrestling for two hours is another! Translate that to the complexities of several hundred adults or more. The best and most practical way to be supportive and understanding of the expectation problem is to learn the priorities of your church. Individual churches vary in their specific emphasis, but all churches must focus on the four basics of church growth. They are evangelism, discipleship, prayer, and assimilation. These are not the high-visibility, high-attraction ministries, but they are the four that will provide sustained growth for your church over the long haul. Support your pastor in his emphasis on these four basics.

DO NOT PUT EXTRA DEMANDS ON YOUR PASTOR'S FAMILY

It is very important for your pastor's spouse to be fully supportive of the church's ministries. But remember, the church hired the pastor, not his spouse. The days of getting a free organist, Sunday school teacher, and women's missionary society director are over. Your pastor's spouse must be free to volunteer for the ministries of her choice. And if your pastor and his wife have young children it is even more important to be sensitive to their needs. There is often undue pressure for P.K.s (pastors' kids) to be perfect, particularly in smaller churches where the kids are more visible. Let the pastor's kids be kids and let your pastor know that you don't expect his children to be superhuman.

A pastor friend of mine told me a story about his six-year-old son. In Sunday school, the teacher expected him to know all the answers to the Bible lesson! Even the teacher didn't know all the answers! Why place such a silly and unrealistic expectation on a six-year-old boy?

Another pastor friend told me a story about his twelve-year-old daughter. His daughter was gifted musically. She loved to play the piano and sing. She also enjoyed playing and singing some of the "pop" tunes of the day, rather than exclusively Christian music. She received great pressure and even some ridicule about playing anything not in a hymnbook or chorus booklet. The teens who weren't the "pastor's kids" also enjoyed some contemporary secular music, but they received no criticism. The ridicule rose to the extent that she didn't want to go to church and began to doubt her faith. "How could church people be so mean to me?" she would ask. She has since grown up and gone off to college. I hope she has found the grace she deserves.

A good rule of thumb to remember is not to expect more of your pastor or his family than you would want him to expect of you.

ENCOURAGE YOUR PASTOR'S FAITHFULNESS TO HIS TIME OFF

Pastors are often guilty of not taking their day off. Most have a six-day workweek to begin with, so it's doubly important that they take advantage of free time for their own replenishment. Occasionally, most professions require long hours to complete a special project, but not on a consistent basis. Dedicated pastors frequently use their off days to meet the needs of people in their congregation, or as a quiet study day for sermon preparation, because the rest of the week has been consumed by the needs of people. Dedication is a noble trait, but this kind leads to ineffectiveness and ultimately to burnout.

As with the rest of us, if your pastor works for extended periods of time without a break, he becomes more susceptible to temptation. This temptation can come in a wide variety of ways, from overeating to an impure thought life.

Long periods of work without rest also cause stress within the pastor's family. Because he is so exhausted, the little time he is home he has nothing left emotionally for his family. If the pastor's family is not healthy, it is not possible for him to sustain a Spirit-filled and fruitful ministry. Fatigue leaves the door wide open for direct spiritual attack from the enemy, and rest is the first step to closing the door. Rest provides the renewal necessary to gain the proper perspective. Rest provides the refreshing that comes from waiting upon the Lord, from whom he will receive strength and guidance.

Because of the emotional stress level in ministry, your pastor needs to take not only his day off on a regular basis, but also his annual vacation time. This is important to his own health and vitality as well as his family's. The bottom line is, an exhausted pastor stunts a church's growth.

You can be a supporter of your pastor's time off in these ways:

- *Encourage him to be faithful to a regular day off.* **When you see him at church, ask him if he took his day off. Tell him that you will be praying that he really enjoys his day off!**

- *Encourage him to faithfully take his annual vacation.* **In my first four years of full-time ministry I never took a vacation. I'm not proud of that, and it was my own responsibility—no one denied me time off. I was simply foolish. It took me those years to learn that I was not only robbing myself and my family, but also my church by not getting the needed time away. Make sure your pastor and his family get an annual vacation in which he doesn't have to worry about the issues of the church. He'll be a better pastor for it.**

- *Institute a sabbatical program to be in effect every seven to ten years of ministry.* **You may not be an official board** member or someone who can vote and make this happen. If not, talk to a leader in the church who can make it happen. You can be a change agent in the life of your pastor and your church by supporting a sabbatical program.

• *Don't call your pastor on his day off.* Emergencies do arise, but only in the case of an extreme emergency do I suggest calling your pastor on his day off. Look at it this way: Let's say your church has 150 members and only 10 percent call on your pastor's day off. That means fifteen people call him in one day for him to take care of their problems, of which at least fourteen can wait until the next day.

• *Be patient and understanding if your pastor cannot make an immediate appointment with you.* Let's say that you do indeed wait a day, and call your pastor with a need while he's in his office. You then discover he can't see you for a week and a half. You are really upset and wonder why it takes so long! I have good news for you. If your pastor wasn't any good at what he does, no one would call him and you could see him any time you want! It sometimes takes a while because there are so many people with so many needs.

The central idea is to remember that God created your pastor with special gifts to lead your church, but he is still just as human as you are. You and your church will benefit by encouraging him to be himself and allowing him to play to his strengths.

STEPS TOWARD ACTION

1. Remember that God created your pastor on purpose with a specific plan in mind. Respect and appreciate all that makes him unique.
2. Recognize and embrace your pastor's humanity by forgiving mistakes, encouraging risk, and telling him you believe in him.
3. Give your pastor permission to be himself.

4. Encourage your pastor to be fully authentic by first being authentic yourself. Practice open and honest communication from the heart.
5. Give your pastor the latitude he needs to be the leader of the congregation.
6. Allow and encourage your pastor to play to his strengths. Learn his leadership style, personality type, and spiritual gifts, then let him focus on those arenas.
7. Be an advocate of realistic expectations for your pastor.
8. Keep focused on the priorities of the church.
9. Don't put extra demands on your pastor's family.
10. Encourage your pastor to be faithful to his time off.

DON'T PICK UP YOUR
MARBLES AND GO HOME

"That was the last straw—it was time to march on 'city hall,'" decided Ken Bute when he was upset with his pastor. "Then God got hold of my heart."

Here is Ken's story:

As a member of my church for eighteen years, I'd weathered the changes, the building campaign, and the crowded parking lots. But this latest decision of Pastor's was wrong. At minimum it was very upsetting.

I didn't understand my pastor's reasoning, and I strongly disagreed with his choice. This time, I determined, he would know about it. It was a risk, but I felt it best to at least meet with Pastor. I wanted to tell him how I felt, why his decision seemed wrong, and how it hurt me.

I'm glad we had that meeting. In it I learned that Pastor was looking to God for wisdom and direction. His decisions were based on his prayerful seeking of God's will. He desired to please God, not necessarily Ken. I also learned why I was so ready to cause a fuss. It wasn't just because of one of Pastor's decisions, or the fact that I was keeping score of some of the little problems along the way. It was really because I was looking to man, not God, to please me and meet my needs.

I have since renewed my commitment to trust God for all things. I can trust Him for godly leaders and the wisdom they need, as well as for my own needs for direction and guidance.

In Matthew 6 God says, "Each day has enough trouble

of its own." I want to be part of the solution and not add to any of the day's trouble. It's with this attitude, where my roots run deep in God, that I'll bloom for His glory.

Ken Bute is a financial officer in a growing company, the father of two great kids, and very lucky to be married to Shannon. Ken and Shannon are mature and loyal Christians who have learned the blessing of keeping their eyes on God.

BE PART OF THE SOLUTION

One hot summer day the air-conditioning had once again gone out in my office. I had just been brought word by Jim Fletcher, a key player on the relocation committee, that "the bird" was back in full force. "The bird" at Skyline is by name a Black-tailed Knat-catcher who single-wingedly has caused significant and complicated delays in the process of the church's relocation. Our future location contains the habitat in which the Knat-catcher builds its home, just so we can have some endangered neighbors. One thing was clear, the Knat-catcher was receiving far more support than the church. That was it! Between the pervasive heat and the return of "the bird," I knew God was calling me to another church.

Coincidentally I visited another church that I thought had "no problems" that weekend. Not only did I observe obvious weaknesses, but I heard the pastor of this "great" church lament about them during the sermon. Yikes, there was *more* than one "bird"!

In my few frustrating moments at Skyline, all I had to do was visit another church on a Sunday and I was instantly convicted of my attitude and acutely aware of how fortunate I was to be in a church as wonderful as Skyline.

I learned two important lessons by visiting other churches: There is no perfect church, and I can either be part of the problem or part of the solution.

Let's begin with the faulty idea of a "perfect" church. It's a lot like the courtship process before the reality of marriage. The young couple are starry-eyed and in love. They are "perfect" for each other. They get married and the first time she finds her best dish towels have been used to wax *his* car, and he finds that she can *legally* say "not tonight, dear," a whole new definition of reality is cast. It really is a shock the first time he sees her without makeup and the first time she hears him make noises she has only heard on farms and in zoos. But they will be fine. With love and understanding they will grow to appreciate all of their differences.

Unfortunately, some couples try to escape to another more promising relationship only to find the new one is not perfect either. There is no greener grass.

The church is the same. As my mom often says, "We're all different; we need to love each other, 'warts and all.'" At the time, I didn't much care for my little sister's "warts," but as I matured I understood the wisdom of my mom's words. The church has "warts" too. It's up to us to grow up and seek to understand one another, not to complain without helping or leave altogether.

There is another matter of a slightly more theological nature. The church is not only imperfect, it was designed for imperfect people. God created the church to be a place for sinners like you and me to be saved by grace through His Son, Jesus. We are then to grow spiritually by learning from other more mature, but still imperfect, believers.

The second lesson I learned is that I can either be part of the problem or part of the solution. I can be part of the problem in two ways: First, I can be personally involved in the causing or the spreading of the problem. Second, and this way is much more subtle—I can do nothing. By doing nothing I'm no more innocent than Pilate was when he washed his hands. I am just as guilty as if I were in the middle of it all. Our church is like our family, it's heaven's local address for us until Jesus returns to take us to our eternal home. Our church needs us to jump in and be part of the solution for whatever problems it may be experiencing. Remember, there is no perfect church, so if you are unaware of any problem, ask your pastor. Offer to help where you can, and pray no matter what.

A young married mom named Sharon came into my office and complained that the nursery was less than adequate on Sunday mornings. She was quite passionate as she listed all the things wrong with the nursery. Then she said the words every pastor longs to hear: "Dan, I want you to know that I love my church, and I'm not here just to complain. I'm here to let you know of a serious problem and to offer to help you solve it. I'm willing to start working this Sunday in the nursery, and every Sunday after if that's what it takes." What a blessing and encouragement! That's the way to do it! (By the way, Sharon did start that Sunday and made a huge impact in our nursery ministry.)

A favorite story of mine illustrates well the idea of being part of the solution rather than part of the problem. Think of each of us in the church carrying two buckets at all times. One bucket is filled with water and the other bucket is filled with gasoline. Every time we come upon a fire (a problem) in the church, we have a choice; either throw the bucket of water on the fire and put it out, or throw the bucket of gasoline on the fire and make it worse. It's always our choice.

DON'T NITPICK THE SMALL STUFF

I saw a great bumper sticker on the back of an old pickup truck. It read: "Don't sweat the small stuff . . . and it's all small stuff." Of course, not everything in life is small stuff, but the point is a good one. Most of the things in life we fuss about aren't worth it.

For example, whenever I hear the word *paint* in a church my blood runs cold. I pray I don't hear the two fatal words, "what color?" More blood has been spilled over the color of paint in local churches than any of us would care to admit.

Young, naive, and full of energy to change the world is a

great way to describe me as I set out to build the Sunday school at Skyline. Part of any successful turnaround is changing the image. Part of our Sunday school image-changing program was to spruce up all the Sunday school classrooms. For twenty-eight years they had been Navajo White. I had no idea of the profound wisdom in this mandate from the maintenance department. Frankly, I thought it was a bit narrow-minded and quite unimaginative. Not only did I remove the "Navajo White Mandate" (which I later believed that God Himself probably recommended), I gave permission for each department of teachers to select its own classroom color. You would've thought I had called a congress to reinterpret the gospel of John.

This one wasn't going away. I'd opened Pandora's box and little did I know it was filled with paint! One particular department had divided itself into the Cowboys and the Indians. The Cowboys wanted blue and the Indians wanted yellow. I was called in to make the decision. I have to tell you, I was strong, decisive—and stupid. I chose yellow. You can figure out the rest of the story. The good news is that the Cowboys did not leave the church, although for weeks I was looking over my shoulder for a lynch mob!

People are people. When given subjective choices, they will defend their choice, no matter how small. Unfortunately, there are times when we all get so focused on the little things that we miss the big picture. In the heat of the moment those things don't seem so small, but if we will stand back and look with a broader perspective we'll be less likely to get stuck in the small stuff.

GIVE UP YOUR RIGHTS

We often define the "small stuff" differently, and this is where the problem starts. But the real issue is inside each one of us. We want our way. It's part of our nature. We're born wanting our way, and the rest of our lives we mature, hopefully, to a more others-oriented viewpoint.

My children are still very young, and though they are wonderful children, on occasion they seem nearly obsessed with getting their way. It may be the topic of what they will wear to school in the morning or how late they stay up that night. It doesn't really matter—the debate is on. As a parent, I've always wanted to know who suggested to these kids that negotiation was part of the deal. My kids are master negotiators. When I hear terrorist stories on the news where hostages are involved, I wish I knew whom to call because I think my kids could negotiate with the terrorists and win. Within thirty minutes I think my kids could have them screaming "Anything you want, please, just leave us alone!"

We can smile when we think of these kinds of stories about children. They are still young and have time to mature. But what about when adults are still behaving like children and demanding their way? They don't yell and scream, but in a more sophisticated manner they still attempt to get what they want.

Jesus modeled a very different attitude for those of us in the church. He gave up His rights.

Philippians 2:1–8 says it clearly:

> **If you have any encouragement from being united with Christ, if any comfort from his love, if any fellowship with the Spirit, if any tenderness and compassion, then make my joy complete by being like-minded, having the same love, being one in spirit and purpose. Do nothing out of selfish ambition or vain conceit, but in humility consider others better than yourselves. Each of you should look not only to your own interests, but also to the interests of others. Your attitude should be the same as that of Christ Jesus:**
> > **Who, being in very nature God,**
> > > **did not consider equality with God something to be grasped,**
> > **but made himself nothing,**

taking the very nature of a servant,
being made in human likeness.
And being found in appearance as a man,
he humbled himself
and became obedient to death—even death on
a cross!

When you join a country club you get special rights and privileges. When you join a church you give up any special rights and privileges. Personally, I believe that the blessings far outweigh the sacrifices, but nonetheless, there are sacrifices. Little things sacrificed on earth add up to big things of eternal impact in heaven. You may give up your right to a close parking spot so that visitors and senior citizens can park more conveniently. You may give up a nice Sunday school room for your adult class so that the nursery can be expanded. Whatever the need, Jesus is saying: Give up your rights.

Music is another hot button in most churches. Contemporary or traditional? Loud or quiet? Free-flowing or pre-planned? Nothing can get people's emotions moving quicker, ironically, than discussing what kind of worship is most pleasing to God! Just the ideas of guitars, drums, and synthesizers are enough to get some churches heated up. Or how about the organ? It's the single most divisive word in any music department in just about any church in America.

Let's go way out on the edge: hands in the air during worship, or hands kept at your side? I wonder what God thinks about all this. The truth is that it's not *how* you worship, but *whom* you worship that matters. God made us all different and gives permission for the "creature" to worship the "Creator" with free will. There is no right or wrong. Support your pastor's decision of worship style. It is impossible for him to make everybody happy in this sensitive area of worship style preference. It isn't biblical or wise to try to make everyone happy. The pastor is called to spend time with God, listen to the leaders, and then make the decision. You are called to offer your suggestions and then support the decision. This is what Paul meant in Philippians 2 when he said, "being like-minded, having the same love, being one in spirit and purpose."

MODEL A POSITIVE ATTITUDE

Attitude is a choice, primarily how we choose to look at life. To one person the glass of water is half empty, to another the glass is half full. Every situation in your church has two perspectives. One is positive and one is negative. Please note that I didn't say right or wrong, but positive and negative. Right and wrong refer to judging; positive and negative refer to perspective.

Larry Clark, my good friend and a faithful member at Skyline, is one of the most positive people I know. One time he was fixing his Volkswagen minibus, and while lying underneath the van the entire contents of the oil pan dumped on his face and chest. Larry quickly scampered out from under the VW and his first response was, "I'm so fortunate the oil wasn't hot!" *Fortunate?* There he stood dripping in black thirty-weight and he felt fortunate? But he *was* fortunate, because that was his perspective.

Larry carries that same attitude into the church. When the music department throws an extra challenge his way, he chooses to see it in a positive light. If you are a skeptic, you may be thinking, *Well, this Larry may be a nice guy, but he's also in denial.* I can assure you he is not in denial. He has, however, chosen to see life in the most positive light possible.

Coming home on a recent trip from Virginia, I was disappointed to discover that my flight was canceled. Through other flight delays the domino effect kicked in and caused a total delay of seven hours in my arrival home in San Diego. I didn't do as well as Larry with my attitude. *Fortunate* was the last word I would have chosen to describe the worst flight day of my life. But no level of frustration could change the airline's ability to get me home on time. The day was lost. And instead of using the time constructively to get something else done, to relax, or to pray, I allowed myself to get frustrated. I lost. Attitude is everything.

Attitude can make or break a church. You can't see attitude, but next to the Holy Spirit, it is the single strongest force within us. Attitude influences our decisions. Attitude shapes our relationships. Attitude colors our feelings. Attitude impacts our behavior. Attitude is powerful. A church with a "bad attitude" is in trouble. How do you know if this is true of your church? You will notice things like a negative atmosphere, little trust, low morale, and possibly a critical spirit among the people. The scary thing is that occasionally this attitude is masked by a sweet and friendly veneer that does not represent how the people really think and feel. A surefire way to test attitude is to listen to what is said *after* an important meeting. I've been in meetings that were filled with praise, prayer, and positive statements only to hear in the hallway ten minutes later (or the next day) the emotionally charged words of how the people really felt.

Brighten Up Your Attitude

There are many helpful ideas to help you possess a consistently positive attitude. The following five principles will not only help you brighten up your attitude but also your church.

1. Understand that attitude is a choice.

No one was born with a bad attitude, and yet so many people wake up in the morning with one. Where does it come from? Tough breaks in life? No, many people who have tough breaks in life have a great attitude. Personal limitations? No, everyone has personal limitations and many people with severe limitations or even handicaps have great attitudes. Attitude truly is a choice.

One of my kids wakes up in the morning with a song and a smile, the other wakes up unhappy because the sun came up again. They are both wonderful kids, but one needs constant coaching in the area of attitude. Patti and I invest our energies on a daily basis to communicate to our "getting happy" child that her attitude will determine the quality of that day. More times than not, when confronted with a picture of what a good day versus a bad day looks like, she chooses a positive attitude. If young children can do this, adults can too.

2. Believe the best in everyone.

The old saying is true, we find in people what we look for. Since no one is flawless, if you look for imperfection, that is exactly what you will find. If, however, you look for the positives, those are what you will find. The principle of believing the best in everyone isn't a naive, pie-in-the-sky concept with no connection to reality. It's a principle that encompasses the truth that everyone is endowed with strengths and weaknesses, and the church is far better when its members focus on each other's strengths. Which do you want others to focus on about you—your strengths or your weaknesses?

3. Give people the benefit of the doubt.

This is a cousin to believing the best of others, but the principle focuses on a specific area of gossip, disagreement, or misunderstanding. So much of life is based on individual perspective that without the benefit of the doubt there is often unnecessary conflict.

In the marriage counseling I have conducted as a pastor, I've seen nearly all of the couples with marriage struggles make progress when they begin to give one another the benefit of the doubt. This means the husband chooses not to assume that his wife's silence indicates unhappiness. Giving the benefit of the doubt means believing the best, taking the initiative to learn the other person's perspective, and making no judgment until both sides are explored and understood.

Give your pastor the benefit of the doubt as well as your fellow members in your church. God will bless your attitude.

4. Go for the win-win scenario.

In any situation where people are involved in a win-lose scenario, one person doesn't really win, and one person really loses. In the body of Christ we are called to unity, not division; cooperation, not competition; generosity, not selfishness. There are no win-lose scenarios in the church. Anytime we "win" where one brother or sister in Christ is concerned, we lose because another part of our family in Christ "lost." Unless all concerned parties benefit, don't do it.

5. Ask, "What would Jesus do?"

"What would Jesus do?" is a question worth answering in most of life's major and day-to-day decisions. Read Philippians 2–4 and discern what it means for you to have a positive attitude as a Christian.

CULTIVATE A TEAM SPIRIT

The very nature of a team involves a group of people coming together to accomplish something that could not be accomplished by individuals alone. It's a unified group effort. In this case the pastor is the coach and the congregation are the players. The team cannot function without both. There are many times on even the best of teams where certain players don't get their way, but they don't "pick up their marbles and go home." The best teams have learned how to work together for a higher and greater good than what their individual selves could accomplish.

The Winning Team

There are five essential traits of a winning team to be followed consistently. As you incorporate these into your life and the life of your church, you will be blessed with positive results.

1. Cooperation.

Cooperation links to attitude and is the first in the building blocks of a winning team. Cooperation is the art of adults with differing opinions coming together in agreement for the sake of a higher cause. Simply put, it's the art of getting along. Moms often call out to their kids, "Can't you guys get along?" Kids in the midst of a squabble often are not able to settle their differences. They haven't yet matured to the point where they have the skills and discipline to achieve cooperation. When adults don't cooperate, however, it's their *choice.*

I remember a church board that was in the process of choosing a computer system. The board was split right down the middle. Fifty percent wanted a big IBM mainframe and 50 percent wanted a PC network system. It was worse than the civil war—brother against brother! No one would budge. The mainframe was purchased, and half the board was furious. A couple of men threw up their hands in frustration and were soon inactive in the church; one eventually left. He picked up his marbles and went home. This is not cooperation. There are many creative possibilities for handling a stalemate like this. How would you handle it in your church?

An important ingredient to cooperation is trust. Mutual trust must be established in order for cooperation to blossom. Trust is best established by extending it without making people earn it or prove themselves worthy of it. If someone behaves in such a way that shows he or she is untrustworthy, then trust is revoked, but not without extensive conversation concerning the pattern of dishonorable behavior first. In other words, first give the person the benefit of the doubt.

Respect is another ingredient for cooperation. It means honoring one another. Respect says, "I value you as an individual." There is a deep and abiding sense of human dignity in respect for one another.

Abraham Lincoln, Orange Scott, and Martin Luther King, Jr., taught our country much about respecting our black brothers and sisters. Parents teach children to respect their elders. Pastors teach their congregation to respect the Word of God.

Once I dealt with two adult Sunday school classes that

shared the same room but at different hours. The class who followed the other class complained that they "trashed" the room before they left each Sunday. I thought they were exaggerating just a little, but I went to check one Sunday. They were right. The room looked as if a bomb had gone off. From the coffeepot to the blackboard, it was a mess. The first class was communicating a lack of respect to both the people of the next class as well as the church property. The good news is that after I sat down with the class leadership they immediately made great improvement.

The third ingredient to cooperation is being others-oriented. The apostle Paul taught in Philippians 2 that we are to put the needs and interests of others before our own. Jesus taught the same principle. This is the opposite of human nature, but an essential principle for cooperation in the church.

Larry Hoagland is a wonderful friend and faithful leader at Skyline Church. He's a professional photographer and is often asked, on a volunteer basis, to take pictures of church events. Many of these events do not fall in a convenient time frame for Larry, but he responds cheerfully, putting his own agenda aside, doing his best to meet the needs of others.

2. Communication.

Churches are built by people talking to each other, especially by talking to those who don't know Christ. Communication is essential. Churches are destroyed when people refuse to talk to each other and damaged when communication is poor.

One of the most common phrases I hear in different churches from a large section of people is "I don't know what's going on." This phrase is a warning light. People who are not up on things are generally down on things. It's not always due to a bad attitude. If someone is left out of the communication loop, he or she will feel left out and soon drop out. If you are a leader it is your responsibility to take initiative to make sure the church body stays informed. If you are not a leader but an involved layperson, ask a leader in the church what the main issues facing your church are.

Good communication involves being open and honest. We must take the risk of letting others into our lives so we can encourage and strengthen each other as well as grow the church. Talk from the heart to the heart.

Good communication also requires that we be inclusive as opposed to exclusive. The church isn't designed to be a gathering of cliques, inner circles, and outer circles. It's designed to be a unified body of Christ in which all the participants are equally empowered with information. Certainly discretion is essential when dealing with confidential personal issues, but the reference here is to all information that concerns the big picture of the church.

Active listening makes up the third part of meaningful communication. Communication is a two-way street, requiring both talking and listening. Do you know someone who seems to do all the talking? Or how about someone who barely says two words every time you're together? Both block real communication. My challenge to you is, practice verbalizing your thoughts as well as listening carefully without interrupting other people.

3. Change-oriented.

Will Rogers said, "Even if you're on the right track, you'll get run over if you just sit there." Growth means change. There is no way for you personally to grow or for your church to grow if change doesn't occur on a regular basis. The change I'm referring to is not mechanical but natural, just like the changes a child experiences as he or she grows up. If the child adapts, growth occurs; if not, the child moves from one conflict to another.

Nothing growing stays the same. Support your pastor in the changes that need to be made for God's will of growth to take place in your church.

4. Contribution.

Winning teams have players who all make an equal contribution. The contribution isn't equal in terms of the actual scoreboard, but in effort. They all give their best. I will focus on ministry contribution in a later chapter, but for now let me say that if you make no contribution of your time, talent, or resources, you really aren't on the team. And God wants you to be on the team!

5. Commitment.

Skydiving taught me about commitment. The door to the plane opened at twelve thousand five hundred feet and it was time to jump. It had always been my practice to wait until the plane landed to get out, but this was to be a very different approach and landing. The instant I left the door of the plane I knew a more profound level of commitment than I had ever known before. There truly was no going back. I was committed no matter what. Traveling at over 120 miles per hour, my next and single most important job was to pull the rip cord by five thousand feet. Success! A safe and relatively soft landing.

Commitment is a fragile thing. I watch our San Diego Jack Murphy Stadium fill with less than committed fans. When the Padres do well, the fans show up; when the Padres don't do so well, the stadium is nearly empty. Sometimes as I look at church attendance in sanctuaries I wonder if something similar is going on. People will call in and ask what the sermon title is to make a decision whether or not they will attend church that morning. Some folks sleep in because they were out late the night before. Church members sometimes withhold their tithe to demonstrate that they are unhappy with something.

How committed to your church are you? Your church *needs* you to help it become better. Commitment is necessary for your own spiritual growth as well as the growth of your church. Your pastor needs your commitment and support in order to fulfill the Great Commission of Matthew 28—to go and make disciples.

STEPS TOWARD ACTION

1. Make it your purpose to be part of the solution rather than part of the problem.
2. Remember, there is no perfect church.
3. Don't focus on the small, nonpriority issues, and keep your eyes on the Lord.
4. Promise yourself and the Lord that you will always use your bucket of water, not the bucket of gasoline.
5. Be open to a different perspective.
6. Make a commitment to possess a positive attitude.
7. Make a commitment to become a strong player, who adds value to the team.
8. Study the five components of a winning team. In which do you need improvement? Write down your plan for growth.

- 4 -
"I'M NOT SURE I EVEN LIKE MY PASTOR"

"It was not until I was able to be totally submissive to authority that the Holy Spirit was able to show me the blessings that God had in store for me through His church," said Jacqueline Bond.

Here is Jacqueline's story:

For a long time I was excited about church, but slowly I began feeling manipulated and I became discontented. My discontent gradually colored my attitude toward my church and pastor. It was difficult for the Holy Spirit to minister to me on Sunday mornings. I had become preoccupied with trying to figure out what the pastor was "really" saying and wanted from me. I thought my frustration with the pastor would cause me to leave the church.

Instead my husband and I committed to pray together to seek God's wisdom and guidance. Through the process of prayer and time God began to soften my heart.

God taught me that I had an issue with submission. I knew I didn't put my trust in someone easily, but I never realized I had an issue with authority. Even though things at church were not exactly the way I would like them, God was perfect and He was using the church to reach me. The one thing I knew through it all was that I was accountable to God for my behavior and my growth. It was a conscious and continual decision to submit to my pastor's authority and ultimately to God.

My pastor was willing to meet with me, and I openly shared my concerns. He acknowledged my feelings and helped me to see what was in his heart. Because of my willingness to be submissive, God has blessed me with a renewed faith in a church family and an incredible love and respect for my pastor, whose desire is to honor God in all areas of his life. My ministry is now truly blossoming, and my joy is greater than ever.

Jacqueline Bond is a dedicated homemaker with three beautiful children. She and her husband are respected leaders in the church and give generously of their time and talent to the ministry there. (Jacqueline's story is real, but her name is disguised due to the sensitive nature of this topic.)

DISTINGUISH BETWEEN CHURCH ISSUES AND PERSONAL ISSUES

Some people just didn't like John. Not many, but there were a few who didn't like John Maxwell when he was the senior pastor of Skyline Wesleyan Church. He had enough experience to know that he couldn't make everyone happy. John also knew that his primary responsibility was to please God, not man. Still, no one enjoys serving and leading known dissenters. Being the overzealous loyalist that I am, I chose to confront some of these folks in love about their issue with Pastor Maxwell. I sincerely wanted to help.

One couple were troubled by how often John talked about money from the pulpit. Though he was very convincing on tithing, many of us "Skyliners" believed Pastor's yearly series on stewardship wasn't enough! This particular couple disagreed, even questioning his personal sincerity. Knowing John's generosity and that he was one of the largest givers in the church, I had great passion about my perspective. I met with the couple and we had a good conversation. Their story told "the story." They didn't tithe. That was the bottom line. They barely gave to the church at all. They were under great conviction. Seeing that I wasn't *after* them but wanted to help, they began to soften. On their own the couple said that John really didn't preach too often on money, but they were so sensitive on the issue that anything was painful to them. Hearing about their financial burdens helped me become more sensitive to their situation. I prayed for their ability to trust God with their finances and become totally obedient to His Word on stewardship. It wasn't about the church or the pastor, it was a personal issue.

In another instance, a sharp and committed woman made an appointment with me about a "concern" in the church. As executive pastor one of my roles was to handle sticky issues that didn't fit under any of the staff pastors' areas of responsibility. Over the phone she shared with me that her concern regarded Pastor Maxwell and me. Normally, we would handle a situation like this by gathering all persons concerned for the meeting. John, though, had some pressing previous commitments that didn't allow for a timely meeting with this church member. So she and I met, and I learned that she was disturbed that at Skyline no women served on the board, as ushers, as leaders in the church, or on the pastoral staff.

I communicated clearly that there were many woman leaders in the church and mentioned that we had two women with great responsibility on the pastoral staff. This didn't help or change her perspective on women in leadership.

She focused quickly on the fact that the church board was all men. I explained to the best of my ability the mind-set supporting this approach to ministry. It certainly had nothing to do with a position against women in leadership. If that was true, why would we have two women pastors? We were going nowhere, even after I pointed out that we have several women ushers.

By that point I could see this wasn't about the church or the pastors, but had to be a personal issue. She opened up for a few minutes and shared how she had been passed over at work for promotions and less qualified men had been selected for the jobs. She also shared that her marriage was difficult at best. Her husband didn't treat her at all respect-fully. Once again, this was a personal issue, not directly about the church or the pastor. It often isn't easy to know the differ-ence between the two. Emotions run high, pride can kick in, the facts become blurred, and the big picture is lost.

CALMING THE WATERS

There are at least five ways to help find clarity on emo-tional and difficult issues in general. All churches have diffi-cult situations. The strength of a church isn't measured by the absence of problems, but by its ability to resolve the prob-lems. The following guidelines will help you bring a greater level of strength and unity to your church.

Make Sure Emotions Are Steady and Stable

One Sunday morning after I taught Sunday school, a guy approached me, wanting to talk. He was furious. I had made a throwaway statement about eternal security that had noth-ing to do with the lesson, but that's all he heard. And as a matter of fact, what he heard didn't represent my theological position at all. He thought he heard me say that a person could lose his or her salvation. (Really, I didn't!) He blew his cork. If steam could come out of someone's ears, his ears would have been whistling!

A wise counselor once told me that if the response is larger than the issue at hand, then the response is about something else. I knew this wasn't about my view of eternal security. So what was the real issue? We talked a long time, long enough for him to calm down and regain a more steady rein on his own emotions. I learned that two of his family members had died knowing the Lord, but in a long pattern of sin and dis-obedience. His reaction was a response to his heartache for his loved ones. And my throwaway remark—irresponsible, in retrospect—threatened the eternal outcome for two of his family members! When I understood the real issue, I was able to help him through the emotion to get to the truth. We talked our way to the foundation of God's grace and the fact that this man was not responsible for his family's spiritual condition.

During the first part of the conversation, while still agitated, he said that he could not attend a church whose pastor didn't believe in eternal security. He finally heard my perspective and calmed down. I then asked him if he really would leave over a conflict. His answer was revealing. He said, "No—not really. Pride might have forced me to leave, but I would have really missed this place."

It's important to think through such issues carefully. I have personally found it to be a great practice to actually write down specific points to gain clarity on the situation. The following questions will help you gain that needed clarity: What is this really about? Can the pastor do anything about it? If the pastor can do something about it, is it his responsibility?

Be Sure of the Facts

California is known for great bumper stickers. One of my favorites is "Don't confuse me with the facts." At times we have all put on blinders for a moment to prevent any more input, even if it was correct input! Sometimes we're overloaded, at other times we might be overwhelmed, but sometimes we're just plain stubborn. In any case we stop short of all the facts. As in a courtroom, a shortage of facts spells disaster. Don't assume anything. Ask questions directly of the people involved. Talk with several people, but not in a way that stirs up trouble. Remember your bucket of gas and your bucket of water. Your conversation must be limited only to those who are involved, and even then, be conducted in a way that builds up the body of Christ.

Check Your Motives

Make sure you have examined your heart carefully. Perhaps there is an issue of insecurity, pride, or even fear involved. A good test for your motives is asking, "Does this seem to be more about me and what I want or about the church and what it needs?" Questioning your motives is different from questioning your character. Motives are usually attached to specific situations and are often short in duration. Character, however, is connected to the heart and is with you in all situations. Therefore, you can have a temporarily flawed motive and still a solid character. Another question to ask is, "What is it that I truly want?" You may discover that you desire the impossible.

Pray Before Taking Action

Before you make your move, whatever that may be, be sure to pray first. Allow some time to settle the issue in your heart. Make sure you have peace about your convictions. If you determine that an issue has more to do with a personal conflict, then release the church and the pastor from any blame or responsibility. Seek wise counsel for your personal situation. If you determine that you do in fact have an issue concerning the church or the pastor, then you must take—again, prayerful—action.

DON'T THROW THE BABY OUT WITH THE BATHWATER

Chuck enjoyed drinking beer. Skyline Church requires abstinence concerning alcohol for all of its members. The bottom line is that if you are going to be a member, you can't drink alcohol. Chuck really loved Skyline and wanted to join but struggled greatly with the position against alcohol. Here's the real complication: In order to have a ministry at Skyline, you also have to become a member. The translation is if you drink, you can't participate in volunteer ministry. Chuck knew ministry was the right thing to do, and he wanted to get involved, but he felt strongly that drinking should not be a condition of membership. We talked about it for months. The issue wouldn't die, and frankly I didn't want it to. Chuck had so much to offer, so much potential for the kingdom, yet all would go undiscovered unless he gave up his right to drink.

At one point he became so frustrated that he nearly left the church over the issue. The irony was that he drank very little. It was a matter of principle to him, just as it was to the church.

Chuck prayed about it, though, and the thought hit him that there is no perfect church. He knew he loved 99 percent of everything about Skyline. It was just this one conflict. He saw, on his own, the big picture and chose not to throw the baby out with the bathwater. He realized that giving up his right to drink was a small sacrifice for the blessing of serving as part of God's ministry team.

I'm not telling this story to make a point about abstinence. This is about seeing the big picture as Chuck did. There will be issues in the life of your church that you will not agree with. Keep your eyes on the importance of staying together as a team. Don't give the devil an opportunity to come in and cause division among you. You might not be happy with the youth ministry or perhaps the music and worship. Remember, there is no greener grass. The best remedy is to pray. Then roll up your sleeves and become part of the solution.

DON'T ATTACK YOUR PASTOR

"You have till sundown to get out of Dodge!" Sounds like something you would hear only in old Western movies, but unfortunately pastors sometimes get this response too. Some churches have reputations as "pastor eaters." These churches are very difficult to deal with as they slowly or speedily "have the pastor for lunch." Though it knows no boundaries, this hostility is more typical among smaller churches whose members have been there significantly longer than the pastor in many cases.

Attacks come in all forms, from anonymous letters to malicious gossip. Innocent pastors have been sued and are out of the ministry today. I'm not implying that the pastor carries no responsibility, but I want to clearly communicate that even denominational congregations who have congregational government (able to vote the pastor in and out) gain nothing by an outright attack on the pastor. Everyone loses and God is not pleased.

Scripture is very clear about building up one another in the unconditional love of Christ. Will you choose to make a positive difference in the life of your pastor and the life of your church, even when conflict exists? I pray that you will!

DO NOT SEEK ALLIES

It's one thing for you to be disappointed or even unhappy with your pastor, it's quite another to gather others to your point of view. Worse than attacking your pastor personally is this idea of mutiny. Many a pastor has walked the gangplank right off his ship, backing away from the swords (not Bibles!) of several key people in a local church. Many of those well-armed members probably had very little passion for or even awareness of dissatisfaction. They were incited to a lynch-mob mentality by just one or two people. This breaks God's heart and dramatically hurts your church.

DESENSITIZING SENSITIVE ISSUES

Sensitive issues left to run their own course often end up with consequences far greater than the actual situation merited. The following guidelines will assist you in dealing with the touchy issues in your church.

Separate Your Convictions from Your Preferences

This first guideline begins with the assumption that you firmly know your deepest convictions. Your convictions must be clearly biblical and bathed in prayer. One great test, beyond the foundation of Bible and prayer, is how easily you might be persuaded to change your mind. The more quickly you change your mind, the less of a conviction you possess. Conviction is not the absence of flexibility; conviction actually increases flexibility. People who base their lives on conviction and principle have very few rules in their lives, and therefore greater flexibility. They are guided by only a few but substantial convictions and principles that are truly nonnegotiable.

One of my church-related personal convictions is that I will only attend a Bible-based, evangelistic church. This for me is a nonnegotiable conviction from which I cannot be budged. There are, however, literally hundreds of ways to preach biblical sermons and share Christianity with nonbelievers. I am totally flexible with all the options as long as they get the job done. I may even prefer one of my own ideas, but I will give up my preference for the sake of the big picture.

You need to separate your true convictions from your personal preferences. When emotion kicks in, personal preference goes up and conviction can be lost. It's a very human response, often triggered by any form of change. I would prefer, for example, that the church service I attend be over by noon on Sunday. But the East Campus worship service at Skyline currently concludes well past noon. I could get upset, talk to others, complain to the pastor, and just be difficult. But that would accomplish nothing, and there is nothing biblical about concluding by the noon hour. God seems to be okay with church lasting past 12:00 P.M.! In other words, it's not a conviction. It's a personal preference. Battles over preferences cause unnecessary casualties.

Make Sure Your Actions Spring from Your Convictions

If you find yourself taking action in response to a disagreement with your pastor, make sure it's based on your personal convictions. This is a relatively simple process of asking, "Upon what core value or conviction am I basing this action?" If you don't know what that conviction is, do not pass go, do not collect two hundred dollars, and do not bother your pastor! Make sure the connection between your conviction and your action is obvious. If you have to stretch to make a fit, then you're probably fighting a battle that is not a priority.

For example, Patti and I are committed tithers. This action

springs from our biblical conviction about tithing. In contrast, let's say I quit the choir because I preferred fewer hymns and more choruses than the choir was currently singing. That's taking action more from preference, and no one benefits.

Have the Courage to Stand on Your Own

The best single test of knowing and acting on your own convictions is your courage to stand alone on an issue. The bandwagon can be a dangerous ride in the church. Whether you are the driver or just along for the ride, you can't yet know if you will stand alone. Think carefully on any particular issue that is troubling you and ask yourself if you would take the same action if no one else stood by your side.

Be Receptive to Your Pastor's Point of View

Always remember there are many members in the church, but only one lead pastor. He can't possibly respond to everyone's desires, even if he tried. Though he will not always be right, it is right for you to support him. Your pastor's idea or opinion may be very different from yours. Be sure to have an open and receptive mind to his thoughts and plans. Your openness and receptivity will increase his! Your pastor has the more difficult role between the two of you. Remember how many people to whom he must be receptive.

SPEAK THE TRUTH IN LOVE

Speaking the truth in love is a principle based on maturity. Ephesians 4:15 says: "But, speaking the truth in love, [we] may grow up in all things into Him who is the head—Christ" (NKJV). *Growing up* is a straightforward way of describing our goal as believers. The previous verse gives the context by contrasting a mature adult to an infant who is easily swayed by the influences of others. Children do not always speak the truth in love. Actually, it's funny to think through the stages of how we teach kids to communicate: First we're happy if our children will just speak. Then we hope it's the truth.

Finally, we as parents try to shape their attitude so their tone of voice allows the truth to be tolerable.

There are three important facets of constructing a solid foundation for biblical communication. Allow these three to speak to your heart.

The first facet is that of *initiative*. Verse 15 says "speaking." Silence or listening alone is not part of successful communication. Maturity requires you to speak up with what is on your heart and mind.

The second facet is *integrity*, which requires complete honesty. Verse 15 refers to "the truth." People of integrity are truthful. Your integrity reveals your character. Your word becomes your bond, and you become a trustworthy person.

Verse 15 also says "in love." We are to speak the truth in or with love. *Intimacy* is more of an attitude than an action. It's an attitude that is others-oriented and involves a close connection. This instructs us as to how we say things, not just what we say.

IF AT ALL POSSIBLE, SEEK RECONCILIATION

Let me liken the church to my first car, a 1962 Rambler. The engine was a flathead six, and it never ran on more than five cylinders the whole time I owned it. One headlight would flicker on and off, and the muffler would occasionally come loose, which sounded like a moose in mating season. There were so many things out of whack on the engine that they caused other parts to overcompensate, overheat, and basically just cease to function. The parts weren't working together at all, let alone in smooth harmony resulting in power and forward movement. I can remember turning the car around and backing up really steep hills because reverse was the only gear low enough to produce the power needed to get up the hill! What a car!

I know some churches that have to back up to go forward. And in nearly every case, there are a few church members causing a major fuss in the "engine room," in this case, the office of the pastor. There is no way your pastor can operate on all cylinders if he has to overcompensate for several misfiring church members in his congregation. He can try some oil, he can use high-octane gas, he can even bring in an expert to try to fix them; but often at this stage nothing short of a complete overhaul will do the job.

In the church a complete overhaul happens in the heart. Much as in a troubled marriage, a change of heart repairs the damage. It's called *reconciliation*. Josh McDowell has said, "It's more rewarding to resolve a conflict than to dissolve a relationship."[1] I believe that with all my heart. Your relationship with your pastor is a special one. It affects many other people and it matters to God. It is possible that you have some differences with your pastor that are simply not going to go away. Your relationship with your pastor and ultimately your relationship with God are far more important than any issue in the church. Realize that your relationship with God is dramatically affected if you are in conflict with your pastor, because it is difficult to focus on peace with God if you are at war with one of His servants.

Restoring your relationship with your pastor is simple, though not always easy. It is simple because it requires only a change of heart. But a change of heart can be difficult. I've outlined three steps to a change of heart:

1. A *change in perspective* is a change in how you "see" things. It allows you to see the positive aspects of a different point of view. It's important to be supportive of another point of view. You may be thinking, *Isn't this perspective thing a two-way street?* Yes, it is, but remember, there is only one pastor, and many, many people in the church. It is impossible and unbiblical for the pastor to try to respond to everyone's opinions and preferences. Usually a change in perspective will fall to you.

2. *Forgiveness* paves the road to harmony. Colossians 3:13–15 says: "Bear with each other and forgive whatever

grievances you may have against one another. Forgive as the
Lord forgave you. And over all these virtues put on love,
which binds them all together in perfect unity. Let the peace
of Christ rule in your hearts, since as members of one body
you were called to peace. And be thankful."

This passage sums up this chapter well. I believe if we all
seriously took this Scripture to heart, churches across America would break out in revival. Might that include your
church too?

3. *A commitment to cultivate the relationship* means being
proactive in the most positive way. Even the best of relationships require care and feeding to remain healthy and growing. You may never be close buddies with your
pastor—frankly, in larger churches that is nearly impossible.
But you can still enjoy a wonderful relationship of mutual
support and shared vision for church growth. Perhaps this
means praying for your pastor more regularly, or writing him
a note of encouragement. It may be just going up to him on
Sunday morning and expressing gratitude for his ministry.
One thing is for sure: You cannot avoid him and be a fruitful
member of your church. So move toward him with the grace
and peace of Jesus Christ. The body of Christ is designed to
function in harmony. Follow Colossians 3:13–15. It works!

DISCOVER THE JOY OF SUBMISSION

Joy and submission don't seem to belong in the same sen-
tence, at least for those of us who are hard-charging and opin-
ionated, but they do. My children, Mackenzie and John-Peter,
are learning at a young age the difference between joy in submission and the consequences of disobedience. The rewards
of a clean bedroom are far sweeter and more attractive than
the privileges lost for a bedroom that looks like the aftermath
of a stampede.

The commandment found in Deuteronomy 5:16 states it
clearly: "Honor your father and your mother, as the LORD

your God has commanded you, that your days may be long, and that it may be well with you in the land which the LORD your God is giving you" (NKJV). The truth is that young children are not often joyful about the decisions we as parents make for them, but we know what is in their best interest. They do possess, however, a greater sense of security that comes from the boundaries parents set.

For adults joy in submission comes because of maturity. We experience joy with Christ that comes from giving up our rights for the sake of the kingdom of God. God is pleased and the Holy Spirit within us communicates a sense of deep and abiding peace in our souls. It taps into the servant spirit within all who are born again into the Spirit of God.

Hebrews 13:17 says: "Obey your leaders and submit to their authority. They keep watch over you as men who must give an account. Obey them so that their work will be a joy, not a burden, for that would be of no advantage to you."

Do you see the similarities between Deuteronomy 5:16 and Hebrews 13:17? Of course, your pastor is not your parent. But he is spiritually responsible for you. He must give an account one day before God as to his impact on your relationship with Him. Not only does the Bible say to submit to your leader, it communicates that there is no value in doing anything different from following him. Seeing this, I have to ask, What good comes to you and the church by not supporting your pastor?

This certainly doesn't suggest that you should never disagree with your pastor or that you become the official church doormat. If you have questions, ask him. If you have a difference of opinion on a major issue, talk it out. But in the end, if you still don't see eye to eye and the conflict is a matter of preferences, not convictions, will you submit cheerfully for the sake of God's work in your church?

In the joy of submission, the key for every adult is discovering what God wants you to learn through it all. Ask yourself what God may be teaching you if you are finding it difficult to submit to your church leadership.

MAKING THE DIFFICULT DECISION

To leave or not to leave? That is the toughest question for any committed member of a local church. I want you to know that I understand there are some very difficult situations in local churches, maybe in your church. You may feel unfulfilled or even miserable, but I believe that ultimately there are very few good reasons to leave your church. If God has made His direction clear, then go; otherwise stay and be an active, cheerful participant of your church team.

You may ask, "What if my pastor isn't living a righteous and moral life?" The first thing to remember is that you are not the judge and jury, God is still in control. And second, Scripture reminds us to take the log out of our own eye before judging the speck in someone else's eye (Matt. 7:1–5).

If you are in a denomination and you have strong feelings about a sensitive issue, you may need to contact a denominational official. But see your pastor in person first, and if the issue is not resolved, go together to his overseer. Don't do anything, however, if you don't have your pastor's best interest at heart. Your responsibility is to help keep the church steady, not stir things up. Remember your bucket of water and your bucket of gas? If you are in an independent church, however, a moral failure without repentance is reason to leave.

Other grounds for leaving include your pastor's not teaching biblical truth. There are some key issues of our Christian faith that are nonnegotiable. While it is very dangerous to start making lists for the purpose of judgment—remember the Pharisees—submitting to unbiblical preaching is worse. Following are some facets of our faith that must be upheld:

- **The Holy Trinity (God the Father, Jesus the Son, and the Holy Spirit)**
- **The authority of Scripture**
- **The bodily resurrection of Jesus Christ in total victory over sin**

- The sin nature of man—judgment will result without repentance
- The free gift of eternal life through God's only Son, Jesus, who was conceived by the power of the Holy Spirit and born of the Virgin Mary

If your pastor teaches anything in contradiction to the basics of our Christian faith, you have reason to leave. The irony is that rarely does anyone leave a church over biblical issues! Rare is the pastor with a moral failure (in the big picture), and rare is the pastor who teaches heresy. People usually leave churches over things such as a relational conflict or personal preference. These are not acceptable grounds for leaving a church.

If you are considering leaving your church, make a wise investment of your time by thinking through the issues carefully. Ask the following questions and write down your answers. You will find much more clarity by seeing your thoughts in print rather than trying to manage them all in your mind.

- **Do you have peace that indicates leaving is God's will?**
- **Have you had an honest, heart-to-heart conversation with your pastor?**
- **Are your convictions so strong that you'd "rather fight than switch" (change churches)?**
- **Are you leaving because it's best for your family?**
- **Have you prayed and sought God's wisdom through Scripture?**
- **Are you dealing with an issue of anger that is not about the church?**
- **Are you leaving for your own reasons, or are you following someone else?**
- **Do you sense that God has directed you to another church?**

Be careful to listen to God's voice through the whole process. He may be calling you to stay even if you have just cause to leave. Good friends of ours in Alabama had been faithful in a church where the pastor was neither teaching nor living all of God's Word—the pastor wasn't tithing. Worse, he didn't care. Our friends had reason to leave but felt God calling them to stay to provide strength for the church. God gave them further instruction: They were to do nothing and say nothing about it! God communicated that He had everything under control.

Our friends obeyed and stayed, though they were miserable. Months passed, and then out of the blue the pastor resigned and was never heard from again. This leading couple were integral in the transition and search for a new senior pastor. God blessed their obedience and the church is doing well. Though they would have personally chosen to leave, they could see that the church was stronger and so were they for holding steady. God taught our friends much and they are glad they obeyed.

My experience guides me to encourage you to stay and pray for a change of heart. You will grow more in the long run and your church will too. Remember, the next church you attend will not be perfect either.

If you have made up your mind to leave, please allow me to offer you the steps for leaving in the right way. This will be pleasing to God and beneficial to you. The following sequence of steps will offer you and your church a mature and dignified parting.

1. Fast and pray before you make your final decision.
2. Do not talk negatively about the church with anyone. (Remember, it's God's church.)
3. Let the pastor know you are leaving but will not cause any trouble.
4. Do not let anyone follow you out of the church—leave on your own.

5. Don't burn your bridges. Leave with an attitude of grace and dignity toward everyone. God may lead you to come back one day!

I want the best for you and your church. If you are struggling, my prayer is that God will guide your heart and bless your church.

STEPS TOWARD ACTION

1. Determine if the situation is a church issue or a personal issue.
2. Keep your focus on the big picture, not just your own point of view.
3. Never attack your pastor. He is God's representative and the leader of your church.
4. If you take a stand, have the courage to stand alone.
5. Be willing to give up your rights.
6. Speak the truth in love.
7. Make a commitment to biblical reconciliation.
8. Choose submission over rebellion.
9. If at all possible, stay and help your church grow stronger.
10. As a last resort, if God directs you to leave, leave in a way that honors God and your church.

TEN KEYS TO CONNECTING WITH YOUR PASTOR

"We have always been very involved at church," explained Marv and Tami McCarthy, "but after forming a ministry connection with our pastor we developed a true heart for and much deeper commitment to God and our ministries. We now have far more fruit and joy in serving the body of Christ."

Here is Marv and Tami's story:

We grew up in a small church where we were very involved—we showed up on Sunday and Wednesday and helped out with a variety of tasks. We taught Sunday school, sang in the choir, and even took out the trash after the church potluck! This was the sum total of our understanding of ministry and illustrated the unfortunately dutiful nature of our relationship with Christ.

After we were married we moved and promptly found a new church home. At first our involvement at church was the same as before. We taught Sunday school and planned to move forward with "ministry" (still duty) as usual. However, we became involved in a Sunday school class that happened to be taught by one of the pastors. As a result, we began to get to know him on a more personal level. We began to see the ministry as he did and develop a heart for God as he had. We realized the importance of a ministry *team*, not just individual players. As this process continued we found that we became more effective in our ministries and developed a joy for them as well. Our spiritual lives began to grow and we developed more of a passion rather than performance for God. We sincerely believe that this would not have happened without the connecting process that took place between us and our pastor.

Marv McCarthy is a chief technology officer of a software development company. His wife, Tami, is a full-time domestic engineer. They have three tremendous children and are very committed to family life. Marv and Tami are gifted Christians who find great fulfillment in serving their local church and supporting their pastor.

BASKETBALL AND CHURCH

As a teenager I loved intramural basketball. I think the ball in baseball was just a little too small for me. I'm sure my batting average would have been higher if the ball was larger—and came across the plate much slower. Basketball provided several of these advantages, yet I had a problem there too. I never "connected" with my coach. Actually, I had a much closer relationship with the bench than the coach. You see, with the bench, I knew its purpose and how we were supposed to relate to each other. It was there to support me and I was there to keep it warm. As for my role on the team, that was not always clear. The coach would not budge from his annoying insistence about my ability to put the ball through the hoop. While the size of the ball was a help to me, the *hoop* was still definitely too small.

The coach confused me by telling me that the "strength of the bench" was critical to the success of the team. I translated that to mean the team played better without me. (If scoring points is an important issue, he was probably right.) But the bottom line for me was that I never connected with him. I'm not saying that I didn't like him—I did, and I appreciated his skill and commitment to the team. I just never felt that I was in the game.

I lamented my story to a friend and received some of the

best advice I have ever been given. He said: "It's not the coach's job to get you off the bench. It's your job." Wow! The coach is there to cast the vision, motivate, teach the game, train you in the necessary skills, and show how you fit on the team. My friend talked with me about becoming more aggressive, practicing harder, talking with the coach, *and* putting the ball through the hoop. It worked. I went from benchwarmer in my first year to starting guard by my third year. I never was approached by a tennis shoe company for an endorsement, but I learned a powerful lesson about connecting with the coach.

This business about "connecting" is widespread. People have shared numerous stories of estrangement with their boss, teacher, coach, and even their pastor. It is important to note here that none of these included relational problems; actually, they all liked each other just fine. Mutual respect was present. Yet something was missing . . . a connection that brings substance, growth, and appreciation to the relationship. *Connection* is defined as purposeful affiliation, belonging, and relationship. The focus of this chapter is to provide a greater understanding of that connection with your pastor.

DESIRE TO CONNECT

As with most things in life, desire is the beginning point of success. You must want it, or it will not likely come to pass. There are three reasons why it is important for you to connect with your pastor.

Your Pastor Is Your Primary Spiritual Mentor

Your personal relationship with Jesus Christ is direct and in no need of a mediator. But the Bible is also clear about the pastor-teacher role that your pastor carries in your life. Your pastor is your "spiritual coach." He is responsible to cast vision, motivate, teach spiritual truths, train you in the basics of your faith, and show you how to fit on the ministry team. Your job is to get off the bench by getting in the game.

Getting in the "game" of spiritual growth is vital. Nothing is more important than your walk with God, and your pastor is the primary influencer of your progress! A lack of connection could result in your remaining on the "bench" of your spiritual life.

Your Pastor Is Your Primary Ministry Mentor

In addition to spiritual growth, God's plan for your life includes personal development in the area of ministry. God wants you to make the greatest possible impact for His kingdom you can according to your gifts. (See Chapter 8.)

Your Pastor Is God's Representative and Leader of Your Church

The fact that you are reading this book tells me that your church is important to you. How much more important do you imagine your church is to God? God has appointed your pastor with the awesome responsibility of spiritual oversight and leadership of the congregation you are part of. Connecting with your pastor is an essential part of the unity of the body in your church. Unity is the single most powerful tool that will help your church reach its maximum potential for God. Your pastor is the one called to point the way and lead the charge. If the people in your church ran in any direction they desired, success (spiritual growth) would never be achieved. But if you all pull together with a unified spirit, under your pastor's leadership, and with God's blessing, there is no limit to the growth potential.

TEN KEYS TO CONNECTING

Key #1—See Your Church with Your Pastor's Perspective

The most natural thing in the world is to see life from your own point of view. It's so normal that unless you make an effort to walk in another person's shoes, so to speak, you may never gain his perspective. Seeing with someone else's perspective doesn't mean you change your views or follow blindly. It does mean that you have an appreciation for someone else's frame of reference and experience that are different from yours. Growth almost always results from broadening your point of view.

Your perspective naturally includes the things that are important to you. If you are looking for a church and have children who are teens or younger, the children's ministry certainly would be at the top of your list. Or perhaps you are a senior citizen, and the seniors program would be of interest to you. You think about things like how far you have to drive to church and what the service times are. Things like parking, worship style, and friendly people are issues at the forefront of your mind.

These same issues are very important to the pastor, but he also has things on his mind like: "Can I make the budget?" "Will the board approve the hiring of an associate pastor?" "Will the congregation support a building program?" "How can we increase the number of first-time visitors?" These questions cause your pastor to operate in a way you may not connect with unless you have some understanding of their existence. I am not suggesting that you become intimately involved in every detail of church operations, but do understand and be sensitive to the fact that the church is a complex living organization in which your pastor is responsible not just for the things of interest to you but for the big picture.

The big picture in all churches involves a commitment to growth, both spiritual and numerical. Your church is either growing or dying. There is no in-between. It may seem to you that your pastor is preoccupied with growth. Good! Growth is biblical, and he is protecting your church against sure death, the result of no growth. You may feel that the building needs paint, or the worship style needs updating, but your pastor is looking through a larger scope. He is not ignoring the needs you care about, but his perspective causes him to reprioritize the list.

Your ability to see your pastor's perspective will greatly enhance your ability to make a strong spiritual connection with him.

Key #2—Know Your Pastor's Vision

Hundreds of churchgoers across America have told me their stories about finding a church they want to attend. The idea of connection always comes up early in the conversation. The person might use a different word, but the idea is the same. If people don't feel a sense of affiliation, belonging, and relationship, they will visit different churches until they do.

"I just never connected with the pastor," is a common phrase. "I liked him well enough, and he seems like he's doing a good job, but I just don't know. Something is missing." I know what's missing! A sense of connection. Knowing your pastor's vision is the place to start in making that good connection with him. To know where he is going, where he is taking the church, enables you to determine if you want to go in the same direction. Knowing the direction of the church enables you to be supportive and follow the vision.

The reason the pastor's vision is the place to begin is because next to loving God and one another, it's the core value and central purpose of the church as a whole. It's like the guidance system on the Space Shuttle that determines the success of its journey. If the trajectory is wrong, the shuttle will end up visiting Jupiter or burning up on an unplanned reentry toward earth. My reference to the pastor's vision is not meant to infer that in his leadership there is no teamwork with the primary leadership of the church. Teamwork is very important, and certain forms of church government have a more participatory style than others. The point is that God has called your pastor and given him the primary responsibility to lead the church. The person with the primary responsibility must lead the way with the vision for the church.

Your pastor's vision will undoubtedly contain in some way the Great Commission found in Matthew 28:19–20. The command to "go and make disciples" is essentially about evangelism and discipleship, which translate into church growth. If this is not the highest priority in a church for you, this is the only area in which I would urge you to reshape your thinking. Children's programs, worship and music, and adequate parking are important. Without a focus on the Great Commission, however, your church will soon lack the spark and vitality that keeps the programs important to you alive.

Connection through vision is the key. The point is to know your pastor's vision, and embrace the call of the Great Commission.

Key #3—Always Be Honest

George Washington left us these words of insight and inspiration on the topic of honesty: "I hope I shall possess firmness and virtue enough to maintain what I consider the most valuable of all titles, the character of an honest man." I trust that you feel the same way. Being an honest person is central to the core of Christian values and character.

When you have an opportunity to talk (or write) to your pastor, maintain complete honesty. The absence of a lie isn't always complete honesty. "Partial truths," as they are popularized today, may seem kinder and more gentle in the moment, but in the long run they do more damage. The damage occurs not only to the one who hears and believes, but also to the one who speaks it, because it becomes easier to lie the next time.

I remember a conversation quite some time ago while I was a pastor in San Diego. While helping Tami McCarthy (the coauthor of this chapter's opening story) find the ministry best suited for her, we discussed her personality in relationship to the personality of a leader she might serve under. I suggested that one particular leader might not be organized enough for her. Tami hesitated, then said kindly but directly, "He is more organized than you are." Those words felt like the prick of a dentist's needle as he numbs you up before drilling. It would have been easier for Tami to have avoided the whole point. Fortunately, however, Tami chose loving honesty, and my ministry received the benefit. Our brief but poignant conversation was both meaningful and worthwhile.

This isn't to suggest that you are to be your pastor's self-appointed dentist, "drilling" him whether he wants you to or not. There may be an occasion, however, where God leads you to speak the truth in love. When this happens, do it. Honesty produces trust, and trust creates an environment conducive to a meaningful connection.

Key #4—Never Give History Lessons

Few pastors in America would have the courage to change time itself, even if only for an hour. John Maxwell did just that. Daylight saving time comes once a year, ready or not. The time change always got the better of a couple of hundred people who ended up missing church. They were disappointed to miss the service, and we missed having them worship with us. I suppose we weren't really a full-service church because we didn't offer a "wake-up call ministry." In any case, John had an idea that scared the staff and leaders to death. He announced that on the Saturday night when everyone was to set their clocks ahead one hour, we would not. The motivation was that you could come to church and not lose an hour of sleep. Plus, you could avoid the confusion of a time change. At the conclusion of church that morning you would then set your clock ahead with the rest of the country.

Personally, I don't think John was that worried about the attendance, I think he just loves a big challenge. (The next year he planned to delay the actual sunrise—just kidding!) Those of us who are rebels by nature loved it, though the possibilities for confusion still scared the peanuts out of us! But no one expressed their concerns to John, everyone just held their breath for the coming Sunday experiment against time itself.

Our concern was the obvious potential for confusion. We

church folk are a funny breed, you know. We receive seventeen hundred announcements, thirty-two mailings, and thirty-seven phone calls for a particular event, and we still ask one week in advance, "Now where and when is that meeting?"

Do you want to know what happened? The good news is that a couple of hundred people came to church who wouldn't have because of daylight saving time. The bad news is that a couple of hundred people never fully understood the idea and went out to breakfast or something . . . in any case, we never saw them! After the event the people began to speak up. Monday-morning quarterbacking is an ugly thing. "I knew it wouldn't work," "We could have done this or that to make it less confusing," and "I'm *still* trying to figure out what time it is!" were some of the comments we heard.

Here's the point about history lessons. They don't do near as much good as advice on the front end. (Plus they are really annoying.) If you think your pastor is about to do something that might not work or possibly be misunderstood, say something on the front end. The important key is to support him even if he decides not to follow your idea.

Key #5—Remember, There Is Only One Senior Pastor

Sam called me wanting to talk, and I could tell something of weight was on his heart. He was a long-term, faithful layman in the church, a tither, and participant in the music ministry. When we met to talk, the first words out of Sam's mouth were, "I don't feel connected to the pastor." At first I didn't understand. We had about twelve to pick from at the time, so I asked, "What pastor?" He explained that he meant all the pastors on staff, but especially the senior pastor. Sam told me about his experience years ago in a little church where he could stop in and visit the pastor at any time. He missed that and felt disconnected spiritually and relationally from the pulse of the church. The bottom line was, he felt left out.

Sam wasn't complaining, he was asking for some insight

on how to connect. So we talked about the place to begin, which is a change in paradigms. A new way to look at the situation was the way to find resolution for it. We talked about God's design for church growth, from which the natural result would be a larger church. Larger churches mean less availability of the senior pastor to the people. The pastor was never intended to be the Maytag Repairman of the church, waiting around for the phone to ring. The pastor must be the leader out in front who sets the direction and charts the course. The pastor's job is to equip others to meet the personal ministry needs of the congregation.

Less availability on the part of your pastor doesn't mean he doesn't care. It means he is taking care of his biblical responsibility to grow God's church. Sam needed to realize that it's impossible for the pastor to give personal attention to everyone in the church, no matter what size it is.

I asked Sam if he consistently met the spiritual and emotional needs of his three family members. Sam is a great dad and husband, but he was honest enough to admit that he couldn't always meet that ideal. (None of us can.) So I then asked him how the pastor could possibly keep up with the entire congregation's spiritual, emotional, and relational needs, let alone hang out waiting for the phone to ring or a visitor to stop by for a chat. Sam understood, and our forty-five-minute conversation helped him begin to see the pastor and the church in a different way.

Still, Sam had a need to connect. I offered him some practical steps to help make progress. The first step, which is conceptual in nature, is to redefine connection. This starts with the paradigm shift we've discussed and includes focusing on a spiritual connection more than a relational connection. This in no way eliminates or devalues the relational connection (your pastor enjoys it too), but refocuses the order of priority. You make a spiritual connection through the pastor's preaching, teaching, and public prayer. Your primary relationships in the church are with the other members. The pastor is the catalyst who brings you all together. He "throws the party" but can't be the center of attention for everyone.

Second, I told Sam to keep in mind that the senior pastor is pulled in dozens of directions every day. I encouraged Sam to seek out a relationship with one of the assistant pastors instead.

Third, I encouraged Sam to think in terms of gratitude, simply being thankful for all he did receive rather than dissatisfied about what he did not receive. I reminded him that it's a better way to live, it pleases God, and he would discover more joy and fruit in his church life.

Key #6—Be Your Pastor's Eyes and Ears

Nobody likes a tattletale. Do you remember when you were in elementary school? For some that wasn't so long ago, for others it was near the Jurassic era. Regardless of when you were in school, the kid who told on others was never voted "most likely to succeed." Actually, he wasn't even voted "most likely to live." Being your pastor's eyes and ears is not about being a tattletale.

It's also not about being a gossip. Gossip has reached near Olympic-performance proportions in some churches. The point is simple: Bring your pastor only the information that is intended to benefit, bless, or build up the people in your church or the pastor himself.

Here's how the "eyes and ears" idea works. Keep in mind Key # 5, "There is only one senior pastor"; no matter what size your church is, your pastor can't see and hear everything, nor does he need to. He does need to know more than he personally can gather on his own. When you see or hear things that matter to the life and ministry of the church, take action!

Here are three actions you might take:

1. You could ignore it.

If it's not productive or destructive, then it's not important. Let it go, and urge others to do so as well. Life is too short to fuss about things that don't really matter.

2. You could take care of it yourself.

If you see something that needs attention, and it's a simple deal, just tackle it yourself. Let's say, for example, you see that the youth van is dirty and is therefore not representing your church well. Your pastor doesn't need to stop what he's doing to wash and vacuum a church van. You can help the church by taking care of it yourself. He doesn't even need to know, except that he may have the keys and you need them!

Perhaps you notice that the nursery is short a couple of workers. You can help by jumping in yourself or recruiting a couple of people to help out.

3. You could inform your pastor.

There are, of course, many things your pastor does need to know, and you need to pass on the information. Let's go back to the church van and say that this time it's not just dirty, but the engine is blown. Even if you think you can fix it yourself, the pastor needs to know before you take action.

Perhaps you heard that someone died, or the deacons were trying to sell the church and you weren't sure your pastor knew . . . tell him! If he already knows, that's great, but you covered your bases. Your pastor needs to know if:

- **The situation requires financial resources. Anything that requires church financial resources needs pastoral approval. (The exception is very large churches where some lay leaders have financial decision-making authority.)**
- **Someone has a deep spiritual need. If it is a spiritual need that neither you nor anyone you know is able to care for, then let your pastor know. (Remember, though, your pastor is not a professional counselor or therapist. Most pastors are not trained for in-depth counseling. It is better for your pastor to refer to trained specialists.)**
- **You don't know how to respond. If you know it's important, but just don't know what to do, first contact one of the elders (leaders) in the church. If that is not successful, then**

ask your pastor. If it is not urgent, you can just leave a message or even drop a quick note in the mail.

Your pastor(s) will greatly appreciate this mature approach to ministry relationships in your church.

Key #7—Focus on the Heart as Much as the Mind

Connecting with your pastor is largely a heart issue. Let's refocus for a moment on one of the reasons it's so important to make this connection: Your pastor is your primary spiritual mentor. He is a spiritual leader who helps guide and encourage you in your growing relationship with God. Your relationship with God is largely a matter of the heart; your obedience will be demonstrated in ways outside the heart, but it originates there. Since spiritual matters resound and root in the heart, it is beneficial for you to make a heart connection with your pastor.

At first glance this can appear difficult without spending large amounts of time with your pastor, and that is not practical. But it's not so difficult. Two things can make a substantial difference. The first is prayer. In Chapter 7 I have outlined for you a great prayer plan to use for your pastor. The more you pray for your pastor in this way, the greater a heart connection you will make. The second is to understand and embrace your pastor's vision for ministry. Take time to know and get involved in your pastor's dreams for the church. These two suggestions are not meant to indicate that you should have no time with your pastor, but simply that the time may be limited, and that doesn't prevent the kind of connection needed between a pastor and his people.

What you think is important, and of course God calls you to think carefully about priorities in life. The heart, however, is where it all starts and where it all finishes.

Key #8—When in Doubt . . . Ask!

"What does the pastor need to get the job done?" "What did the pastor mean by that?" "How does Pastor expect us to do that?" are common questions from members of a local church. The irony is that a very large number of these church members, when asked if they've talked with their pastor about the issue, respond with a quiet "No." I don't want to sound cantankerous, but I have often wondered, *Why are you asking if you don't really want to know?* If you really want to know, ask your pastor. A quick phone call, brief letter, or maybe a short appointment would take care of it.

Several years ago while I pastored at Skyline Church, a young couple approached me with great concern. They asked if I had plans to leave the church in the near future. I assured them I did not and thanked them for asking me directly. Here's the interesting part: They had been concerned about this for more than a month but had never asked me! They worried, asked a few others, stressed, and stewed. They said they were even getting a little angry that I was leaving, but never asked me!

Another couple were very worried because they heard that Pastor Maxwell "had cancer or something." There was quite a crowd around John after the church service one Sunday morning, so this couple approached me instead, hoping for some clarification. I assured them that it was a false rumor and thanked them for their prayers. I asked how long they had worried about this and they replied, "For three weeks." In three seconds it was cleared up. Just ask!

Key #9—Make Sure You Have a "Good Connection"

Have you ever made a phone call and the connection was so bad you could barely hear the other person? The sound is a cross between sandpaper and a cat with its tail caught in a door. It's definitely irritating, makes words difficult to understand, and greatly detracts from the enjoyment of the conversation. It is a mystery to me. I can call Japan, Bolivia, or Africa and have crystal-clear sound, then call next door and . . . I'll let it go for now.

Whether it's with your best friend, your children, a

coworker, or your pastor, few things in life are better than a good connection. Clear communication, which requires the ability to both speak and listen, is essential. When every other word is broken up by a variety of interferences, communication breaks down. Communication needs to be both clear and two-way. The fruit and joy that result from such a connection are something to be grateful for and not taken for granted.

Key #10—Take the Time

Everything worthwhile in life takes time. I met my wife at church in 1978. The moment she saw me she was smitten. Though she chased me with the determination of a tiger after its prey, I took some time before I gave in. (She tells the story with a slightly different slant, but this is *my* book.) Despite my creative imagination and clever charm, it has taken time for our relationship to blossom to the depth we enjoy today.

Education, relationships, special projects, rearing children, health maintenance: They all require large investments of time. Sacrifice the investment and you forfeit the blessing, or at least end up with less than the best. The church is no different, nor is the process of connecting with your pastor. I have never understood how people, while "shopping for churches," can make a determination in one or two visits. I suppose there are churches in which things are so different from what you expect or desire you would drop them from your list immediately, but on the other hand, every pastor can have a bad hair day. Take some time to make your decision.

If you have been there for some time, ask yourself if you have done all you can to connect with the pastor. If not, take some tips from this chapter and enjoy more fully the church God has given you.

──STEPS TOWARD ACTION──

1. You must possess a desire to "connect" with your pastor.
2. Take the initiative to see your church through your pastor's perspective as well as your own.
3. Make sure you know your pastor's vision.
4. Never stray from the truth.
5. Give your pastor current events, not history lessons.
6. Don't forget that the pastor is greatly outnumbered.
7. Be your pastor's eyes and ears.
8. Focus on the heart as much as the mind—that is where God does much of His work.
9. When in doubt, ask!
10. Remember that everything worthwhile takes time, and be grateful for the blessing of a great connection with your pastor.

THE POWER OF PRIORITIES

"If we don't prioritize our own lives, we never get to the important tasks," Jeff and Phyllis Boaz told me. "God has allowed us to see how valuable that concept is in the life of a church, and how motivating it is to be a part of a congregation that shares the load."

Here is Jeff and Phyllis's story:

God brought growth to our lives through different church experiences. At the first church we attended, the focus was a weekly salvation message. Phyllis and I knew evangelism was important, but the other priorities of ministry were never developed, so we never really grew—and neither did the church. People who were already saved began to go elsewhere and no one was left to shoulder the load. We wondered if this was all there was to the Christian lifestyle.

Circumstances took us to another city and a new church. The pastor there focused on member visitation to an aging congregation. God had gifted him in this area, and we would have gladly pitched in to share this work so he could develop other areas of ministry. We offered to help, but our ideas found no takers. We were discouraged when the church didn't reach out to the community, and as result, stopped growing.

God then led us to a dynamic, growing church where the pastor understood priorities. We were greeted warmly our first day there, the pastor preached from the Word, the music was offered as worship, and Sunday school was taught by those with a passion for living for God. The pastor was a leader who knew he couldn't do it all himself and allowed others to share the ministry.

> We felt a connection to the church and realized that by
> focusing on priorities, we could grow ourselves and
> really make a difference by using our gifts as part of a
> successful team. Church became alive for us, and we
> were ready to be part of a life-changing ministry.

Jeff Boaz is a marketing manager in the banking industry. He
and Phyllis, his high school sweetheart, have three teenage boys.
Jeff and Phyllis are a dedicated Christian couple who have
served with excellence in many ministries of the church.

THE TWO SIDES OF THE PRIORITY COIN

"It can't be 5:00 P.M. already! Where has the day gone?"
Sound familiar? Have you ever come to the end of a day and
asked yourself, "What have I accomplished?" This is common
among people in the workforce, homemakers, students, even
those who are retired or independently wealthy. Often even
in a whirlwind of activity there is little or no productivity. The
key is not necessarily working harder, but working smarter.

I have learned over the years that there is quite a difference
between knowing something and doing it. We all know how
to improve certain areas of our lives but fail to act on them. I
know, for example, that one of my chosen and biblical priorities in life is to invest quality and quantity time in my children. Both of my kids love the time we play together, and I
know that God is pleased by the love expressed through our
time together. But knowing isn't enough.

Unless I take action on that knowledge, the knowledge is
nearly useless. Because of this I have made a commitment to
regular "date nights" with my kids, curtail my travel, and
have an accountability partner to check on me. Why all this to
do something I say I want to do? Because the demands of the
nonpriority things in life are more forceful than those of the
priority things in life. The unimportant things will always
scream louder than the important things. The squeaky wheel
gets the oil.

THE PRIORITIES OF THE CHURCH

The church is notorious for not tending to priorities. Too many churches focus on things like printing the bulletin, selecting carpet color, and deciding what film series should be run on Wednesday nights during the summer. While things like this are not completely unimportant, they are a long way from top priorities.

One pastor friend of mine mows the church lawn every week. I appreciate his servant's heart and his financial commitment to saving the church money, but his time is not well invested. Does the lawn need to be cut and cared for? Absolutely, but a volunteer can do that just as well. The pastor needs to tend to the higher priorities in his church.

Another pastor I'm acquainted with does all his own secretarial work. I certainly understand tight financial situations, but every church in America has at least one person who would volunteer to help the pastor with secretarial and administrative tasks. This dear pastor spends countless hours a week typing letters, stuffing envelopes, making flyers, and updating records. My heart hurts when I think of the ministry he could be performing. Administrative duties are important and need to be done well, but they can be done by someone else.

I could tell you dozens of stories like these, but it's more important to tell you about the top priorities in your church. My hope is that you respond in two ways. First, that you volunteer to help your pastor with some of the things he doesn't have time to do. Second, that you keep your efforts and energies focused on the priorities of the church. These two responses work in tandem. For example, if you are helping your pastor with church property issues you are freeing up his time to pray, win people to Jesus, write sermons, and train leaders. If you are helping with administrative office work, you can have a direct impact on a key ministry in the church.

I'm not saying that you should not volunteer with the priority ministries. My desire is to show you how things in the church interrelate, and which ones have the greatest impact on your church. (The following are not listed in order of importance.)

Priority #1—Leadership

I believe, as John Maxwell teaches, that everything rises and falls on leadership. John defines *leadership* as "influence." Leadership isn't easy, but it's easy to know if you are a leader. Simply ask yourself the question: "Is anybody following me?" If no one is following, you are not a leader. The good news is that if only one person is following, you still qualify as a leader! The issue is not how many are following, but the *result* of your influence on those who are following you. Are they more like Jesus? Are they more mature in their faith? Are they better equipped for ministry and life in general? How many you influence is as much a matter of God's sovereignty as is your personal giftedness.

Let's take a moment to discuss your leadership profile. Consider the following three profiles and see where you fit.

1. Natural leader.

Some people are born leaders. They just get out of bed in the morning and people follow them. People migrate toward natural leaders, want to be like them, and will help them do nearly anything. Natural leaders are visionary. They have dreams they believe in and can't be silenced about them. They tend to be out-front, trendsetting, and risk-taking. Natural leaders usually have good people skills, are self-motivated, and they're often asked to head up projects, be part of committees, and organize teams of people.

Does this sound like you? You may be a natural leader. If so, you have been gifted by God and I want to encourage you to increase your influence for His glory.

2. Learned leader.

Not all leaders are born leaders; some emerge with latent potential. With the help of a strong leader who is willing to mentor or oversee your mentoring, it is amazing how fast you can grow in your skills and abilities. While I have some natural gifts, I am more of a learned leader. John Maxwell has taught me, and it's not only exciting to see the results but a privilege to pass them on. As a learned leader, on several occasions I have successfully mentored natural leaders! What a blessing to mentor others who start out from a place in life behind you and then pass you by. I love being a coach!

Many of the characteristics of a learned leader are the same as those of a natural leader, but less intense and obvious. There may also be an area or two of deficiency that need to be identified early in the process. This is not a problem unless it is not identified and therefore not improved upon.

Early in my development as a leader, John identified my people skills as a problem. He told me he knew I loved people, but I needed to learn to express that love. Without expressing my caring for people, some folks, John believed, wouldn't know for sure if I even liked them! I knew I did, but I had to learn to slow down and, as John would say, "walk slowly through the crowds." Today, I'm known as highly relational and a people person.

The point of this brief story is that learned leaders can grow tremendously and come to a place of life-impacting leadership, but they need to have at least a small seed of ability to work with. Even the best of artists need some raw material. The first step is for you and your leadership mentor to identify the seeds of raw material that can be guided into fruitfulness. Good mentors can see potential that even you cannot see, so don't sell yourself short. Find a leader, get as much time with him or her as you can, and grow—grow—grow!

3. Non-leader.

If you are not a leader, you're not a second-class citizen. Don't ever let anyone cause you to feel as if you're less than someone with different gifts. God has designed the body of Christ to have many different parts, and obviously not all can be leaders. The truth of the matter is that only about 10 to 20 percent are gifted for leadership. There are many people in the church who are "leading persons," but not necessarily leaders. Here are some common examples:

- **A talented singer who blesses the congregation with beautiful solos**
- **A gourmet cook who creates the most delicious food imaginable**
- **A wealthy businessman who is financially generous to the church**
- **A brilliant teacher who communicates biblical truth in a powerful way**
- **A gifted craftsman who can do nearly anything with his hands**

These people may stand out in your church, but they are not necessarily leaders.

Do you remember the acid test of leadership? Is anyone following any of these people? If you determine that you are not a leader, then your role is to support your pastor in his role of leadership. You can do this in three primary ways: prayer, volunteer service, and representing him well to others.

If, however, you sense that you are a leader, ask God to confirm your gift of leadership. Invest quality time in prayer asking God to show you in different ways His confirmation of blessing and giftedness in leadership. He can do this in a variety of ways, such as your receiving invitations to organize projects or lead ministry teams; people becoming very receptive and responsive to your ideas; your having a sense of vision and mission, and seeing fruit (results) from your ministry. You may also feel a quiet confirmation in your spirit, a restlessness when not leading, and a passionate hunger to grow as a leader. You may also experience affirmation by having other proven leaders recognize your ability.

If you find items in this list are true for you, talk to your pastor about opportunities for you to grow as a leader. As you begin to see your leadership emerge, it is very important that you get all the leadership training you can. Your pastor is aware of leadership books, tapes, and conferences. Ask him which would be appropriate for you. Perhaps your pastor will mentor you in a group setting or suggest alternative mentors. This decision is up to your pastor, and you need to trust his judgment. If he is not able to train you personally, there are many directions he can point you in for your growth in leadership.

At this point, also talk to your pastor about how you can serve as a leader. On-the-job-training in leadership is available in every church. Find out where you can serve as an apprentice leader. Note that the key word is *serve*. Don't announce to your pastor, "I'm a leader, where are my people?" It's important to grow equally as a servant as well as a leader. For example, your church may already have a head usher; perhaps you could serve as the assistant head usher. Or maybe your church has a Sunday school superintendent whom you could serve as an assistant.

Trust your pastor about placement in leadership positions. Even as a leader, your role is to serve as a support to the pastor. You may need to help in an area that is not your first choice but where you are greatly needed. Say "yes," even if temporarily. You could serve for six to twelve months in the area of greatest need, then change to the ministry of your choice. While you are in your "second choice" ministry, don't just mark time. Do your best as unto the Lord, and learn all you can.

Make a commitment to realize both fruit and joy from your leadership. Leadership should be fun. It's not always easy, but it is enjoyable. The joy comes from seeing the fruit. The fruit is a result of the combination of God's blessing and your giftedness. There are difficult times in positions of leadership when you may not see much fruit, and times when it doesn't feel like much fun, but the big picture is the key. When you stand back and look at the whole, do you see fruit and joy? If not, you may need to change your place of leadership or reevaluate your abilities. Perhaps you need more training or experience in an apprentice role.

Finally, make a commitment before the Lord to lead for His glory. You must address the issue of power and authority. As a leader, regardless of how much or little is entrusted to you, some power and authority will be in your hands. This influence is not yours. It belongs first to God, then to the pastor, then to the church as a whole, and last to you. In other words, your authority is borrowed. You are a steward of heavenly authority, and you must always use it for the good of others rather than self-interest.

I have watched power go to some people's heads. Figuratively speaking, say I put someone in charge of the paper clips. Heady with his new authority, he locks them up. He becomes the paper clip sheriff and it takes a form filled out in triplicate to get one. Others I've seen have been true servants, seeking only to add value to others' lives. This is the kind of leadership that brings glory to God.

Priority #2—Unconditional Love

This priority of the church I have learned about most from my kids. They have taught me much about both how to give and receive love. I began understanding unconditional love when I changed my kids' diapers and sat up with them all night because of a colic condition. (I'm no longer convinced that colic is an official medical condition as no doctor has ever been able to adequately diagnose or prescribe anything for it. They just say that in about twelve weeks "it should pass." Three weeks into the twenty-four-hour screaming, we needed promises not likelihoods!)

I also understand unconditional love because my family loves me no matter what. It's one thing to hear or preach great sermons on unconditional love, but to experience it brings a life-changing power to the truth. I'm sure that's why our salvation makes such a huge impact. We realize that Jesus loves us no matter what, and we can't help but be radically affected by that truth. Our responsibility as Christians who are part of a local church is to pass on that unconditional love to people both inside and outside the church.

The basis for the principle of love without limit is found in Matthew 22:37–39, and is known as the Greatest Commandment. Jesus said, "'Love the Lord your God with all your heart and with all your soul and with all your mind.' This is the first and greatest commandment. And the second is like it: 'Love your neighbor as yourself.' All the Law and the Prophets hang on these two commandments."

There are hundreds of passages on this topic, but one of the best is found in 1 John 4:7–11:

> **Beloved, let us love one another, for love is of God; and everyone who loves is born of God and knows God. He who does not love does not know God, for God is love. In this the love of God was manifested toward us, that God has sent His only begotten Son into the world, that we might live through Him. In this is love, not that we loved God, but that He loved us and sent His Son to be the propitiation for our sins. Beloved, if God so loved us, we also ought to love one another.** (NKJV)

According to the passages, God's love must be expressed in three dimensions:

Love God.

Love God with all your heart, mind, and soul. You are to love God more than anything else in the world. Here's a tough question: Can you think of anything you love more than God? Try it this way: Is there *anything*, including a person, that you would not give up for God? With this perspective, the command to love God becomes a huge challenge. But it isn't in a negative sense, because it's an incredible privilege to have such a loving God who *desires* a relationship with you.

The primary way we show God our love is through obedience. Reflect on Jesus' words as recorded by the apostle John:

> **If you love me, you will obey what I command. . . . If anyone loves me, he will obey my teaching. My Father will love him, and we will come to him and make our home with him. He who does not love me will not obey my teaching. These words you hear are not my own; they belong to the Father who sent me (John 14:15, 23–24).**

Obedience to God usually occurs progressively. First, you obey out of fear. Punishment and consequences are your primary motivation. Second, obedience comes from a sense of duty or obligation. You obey because you know it's right. You obey out of character and discipline. Then finally, you obey out of sheer love. You want to please God. It is your delight to bring joy to the Father. It's important to note that no one lives continually at the highest level—levels one and two never disappear. The goal is to live at the third level as much as possible. At which stage of obedience do you live most of the time?

Our children are occasionally less than angelic. They are good kids, but from time to time they like to push the limits, to see what they can get away with. From negotiating bedtime to outright defiance in picking up their toys, they are not always quick to obey. I have tried to make theological sense of this. Does the disobedience mean they don't love "the father"? In that moment, I think they don't. That was hard on my ego until I figured out what was going on. They didn't stop loving me, but in that moment they chose to love themselves more. When they become selfish and want their own way, they are not concerned with the will of their father. I think all of us do that with our heavenly Father at times. We love ourselves more than God and demand our way. That is disobedience in a nutshell. Our goal is to mature in our love to a point where disobedience is less and less frequent and love is more consistent.

Love yourself.

Though you are not to love anyone more than God, you are to love yourself. God knows that deep down inside no one hates himself. Unfortunately, unresolved issues in one's past often cause a great deal of self-destruction and require professional counseling by a qualified Christian therapist in order for self-love to be restored. Self-destructive behavior breaks the heart of God and the will of man.

I'm not a therapist, but I know one of the core principles to the foundation of a healthy love for yourself, and that is forgiveness. A healthy love results from thinking of yourself the same way that God does. He forgives the sin and loves the sinner. If we treat ourselves the same way, we will be neither egotistical with self-love out of control, nor self-loathing, without a healthy regard for ourselves.

God gives His forgiveness freely out of His love for us, but many Christians find it difficult to forgive themselves. If this applies to you in any way, I want to give you a powerful truth that will help: God doesn't love you because you are valuable—you are valuable because God loves you. There is a huge difference. If God loved you because you are valuable, then every time you were less than fully obedient He would no longer love you. That's impossible because God's love is unconditional. Your value resides in the fact that God unfailingly loves you. That fact never varies. Since God sees fit to love and forgive you, you have a foundation upon which you can learn to love and forgive yourself.

Love others.

First love God, then love yourself. You cannot love others without these two in place. You can't give out what you don't first have inside. If you truly love God with all your heart, mind, and soul, as you love yourself, you will be highly motivated to love others. As the apostle John wrote, "Dear children, let us not love with words or tongue but with actions and in truth" (1 John 3:18). Talk is cheap. Scripture says we must put action behind our love. Loving others is about intentionally giving yourself away for the benefit of the other person. Loving others is part of God's plan for you that will bring you great eternal rewards and joy.

Priority #3—First-Time Guests

I love watching first-time guests pole-vault over church members who have parked themselves in *their* aisle seat. These church folks refuse to move from their beloved and preordained places in the pew. This could easily become an Olympic sport. I can see it now, guests Gary and Gena, in the Couples Pew Pole-vaulting event, will attempt a double back-flip with a twist. And here are the scores. . . .

Equally fun is watching the slightly more sedentary Olympic event of head-turning. This event is performed by the church members. When a first-time guest walks down the center aisle, the church member cranks his or her neck in paranormal contortions and stares at the visitor with an expression that says, "You aren't one of us, are you?"

When it comes to church growth, next to a new convert, nothing is more important than a first-time guest. You can support your pastor and build your church by becoming visitor-friendly. This involves both bringing them in and making them feel like kings and queens once they have arrived.

There are two things you can do to help bring in more visitors. First, develop relationships outside the church. Make a list of several friends, family members, and acquaintances who are not churchgoers with whom you can purposefully cultivate relationships with the ultimate hope of making a spiritual impact. Do some fun things together, help them with a project, send an encouraging note. Even if they remain uninterested initially, don't stop being a friend to them. Love unconditionally—that's the model we have from Jesus. This doesn't mean you have to invest huge amounts of time with those who are not as responsive, but remain available to them.

Second, make a commitment to become a "bringer." Not everyone is an evangelist, teacher, counselor, and so on, but everyone can become a "bringer" of people to church. As you develop relationships outside the church, God will direct you to the ones who are ready to be invited. Invite them. It's as simple as that. You are not responsible for their answer, and don't take it personally. Your job is to make spiritual things accessible. You can do it!

Let me be direct and ask, When was the last time you invited someone to church? I don't ask to inflict guilt or overwhelm you. I just want to encourage you to get started. If you are not strong in the area of bringing people to church, make a goal of inviting one person or one couple in the next thirty days. Take this challenge in bite-size pieces. If you succeed in bringing just two or three people to your church in one year, that is great. Can you imagine if everyone in your church brought just a few people this year? Don't get discouraged if it takes several invitations to get one visitor. Be faithful and enjoy God at work in the lives of people.

When your friends do come, treat them as honored guests. Remind yourself that Jesus died for them—that's how important they are to God! Make them feel special. Be friendly and include them in the events of the church. Give them the best parking spots, and move over in the pew so they can have the best seats. Invite them to your Sunday school class or small group. Pray for them and let them know you appreciate them and hope they become part of your church family.

Priority #4—Evangelism

Few things in the church cause more fear than the word *evangelism*. Faces pale and blood runs cold when the pastor asks for volunteers to share their faith. Pictures of snarling dogs, slamming doors, and knocking knees come to mind when we're confronted with the idea of communicating the gospel of Jesus Christ. But it doesn't have to be that way. Evangelism can be a natural part of your lifestyle.

Let me give you a simple plan based on Jesus' teachings:

You are the salt of the earth. But if the salt loses its saltiness, how can it be made salty again? It is no longer good for anything, except to be thrown out and trampled by men. You are the light of the world. A city on a hill cannot be hidden. Neither do people light a lamp and put it under a bowl. Instead they put it on its stand, and it gives light to everyone in the house (Matt. 5:13–15).

Here are two simple acrostics for *salt* and *light*. The first describes the qualities we are to have. The second is a useful evangelistic tool.

Salt

Sensitive to people's needs. Be observant of and sensitive to the needs and problems of people around you. Ask God for opportunities to be a friend to others. Live a "salty" lifestyle so people want to know why your life's different—not problem-free, but exhibiting inner peace and confidence.

Available to share your faith. Ability begins with willingness. You must be willing to share your faith when God presents opportunities. The key is committing to witness *before* God provides the opportunity. The more available you are, the more God will use you.

Listen carefully beyond the words people say. Listen beyond people's words to their hearts. Sometimes what's spoken between the lines is more important than the actual words. Listen for needs and desires, and use them as opportunities to introduce Christ as the answer.

Turn the conversation to Christ. This is the key—and it's also the place where many folks bail out and call their pastor. But a pastor doesn't have what you do: a relationship with that person. Besides, God wants *you* to "pop the question." Tell people about Jesus, and ask for a response. It's not your job to save them, only to share your faith and give them an opportunity to respond.

Light

Love of God. God loves you unconditionally. He accepts you just the way you are. Use John 3:16 here. Most people are familiar with it but need further explanation.

Inner faith in God. You must believe that Jesus is the Son of God and died for your sins. Believing means trusting in what He says.

Gift of God. You must receive the gift of God, which is His Son, Jesus Christ. There is nothing you can do to earn eternal life. It's a gift given to you by the grace of God.

Hope for eternal life with God. Faith in Jesus Christ promises you eternal life in heaven. The life-changing relationship you begin with Him now continues for all eternity. Nothing can change that.

Trust God today. You need to make a decision. There is no push or threat here, just a loving invitation to trust God today for the promise of His Word. Will you accept Jesus into your heart today, be forgiven of your sins, and follow Him the rest of your life?

Evangelism is the core of your church's mission. Your efforts will encourage your pastor, grow your church, and please God.

Priority #5—Maturity of the Believers

The writer of the book to the Hebrews has blunt words for us all:

> **For though by this time you ought to be teachers, you need someone to teach you again the first principles of the oracles of God; and you have come to need milk and not solid food. For everyone who partakes only of milk is unskilled in the word of righteousness, for he is a babe. But solid food belongs to those who are of full age, that is, those who by reason of use have their senses exercised to discern both good and evil (5:12–14 NKJV).**

There is no beating around the bush in this passage! We are called to make progress in our spiritual growth. Whether through our personal devotions, one-on-one discipleship, or learning from our pastors' sermons, the Lord wants us to grow.

Dave Marlow, father of five, businessman, husband, and active member in his church, finds time to invest in his spiritual growth. Dave and I have been friends for years and we have often talked about the need for a daily time devoted to our walk with God. Dave has been an encouragement to me in his discipline and commitment to the Lord. He knows that talk doesn't get the job done, only action. Dave is a runner (something I've never understood for people who own a perfectly good car) and likens the discipline of a runner to the discipline of a Christian. Runners must intentionally pace themselves so they can go the distance. Runners need a plan, a certain course, a time, and a routine for each week. Running in spurts, a few days on, a few weeks off, doesn't produce the desired results of fitness and health. The same is true of sporadic devotions—they do not produce the spiritual health we need. Only a steady diet, a plan, and a set course of progress will ensure our spiritual growth.

I would like you to take a few moments to reflect on your spiritual growth in the last six to twelve months. List the areas in which you have grown, and one or two areas where you would like to continue your growth. What actions can you take to improve in these areas?

Embracing these priorities along with your pastor ensures that all your activity will also be productivity.

STEPS TOWARD ACTION

1. List your personal priorities.
2. Write out an action plan to accomplish your priorities.
3. If God has called you to spiritual leadership, commit yourself to growing as a leader.
4. Love God, love yourself, and love others.
5. Make a commitment to become a "bringer" of people to church.

6. Treat your church guests as if they were kings and queens.
7. Share your faith as God gives you opportunity.
8. Implement a spiritual growth plan for yourself.
9. Support your pastor's efforts to keep these five priorities at the top of your church's priority list.

THE "ON PURPOSE" PRAYER PARTNER

"My prayer life was practically nil when I sensed God calling me to pray for my pastor on a regular basis. I wondered if God had the right person!" admitted Fred Rowe. "I had no idea how much blessing was in store for me."

Here is Fred's story:

> I knew from the time I became a Christian that praying for others was an important part of what believers should do. The only problem was that I never seemed to be able to get around to actually doing it. Prayer was difficult, dry, and above all, boring.
>
> Then I sensed during a prayer time at church that God specifically wanted me to pray for my pastor on a regular basis. It was in obedience to this call that I set out to learn all I could about prayer. I listened to tapes and read books on the subject, was mentored by a prayer leader in the church, and set aside an hour a day, early in the morning, to pray.
>
> What had started out as drudgery turned into a rich relationship with the Lord. My growth in Christ accelerated as I spent time in prayer. I started to see answers to prayers that could have come only from God.
>
> As I prayed for my pastor, God changed my heart toward him. Instead of being critical of his weaknesses I found myself asking God to lift him up and strengthen him far beyond his abilities. When God started to answer those prayers, my pastor was blessed, I was blessed, and the congregation as a whole was blessed.

There is nothing more powerful or more loving that I can do for my pastor than pray for him.

Dr. Fred Rowe is a clinical psychiatrist, who is married to another doctor, his lovely wife, Susan. Together they are raising three active boys and contribute regularly to the church's prayer ministries and leadership responsibilities. Their commitment is a blessing!

ESTABLISH YOUR OWN PRAYER LIFE FIRST

I can't imagine ministry without prayer partners today, and yet for the first several years of my ministry I had none. The difference is obvious. There is more power, more freedom, more fruit, and more joy. It's a win-win situation. As a pastor I was more effective, and the prayer partners experienced spiritual growth and the blessing of God.

Praying for your pastor is essential to his ministry and the growth of your church. Without strong and consistent prayer support, your church's ministry efforts lead ultimately to fatigue and frustration rather than fruit and fulfillment. The foundation of your ability to faithfully pray for your pastor and for your church rests in the maturity of your own prayer life. God honors all sincere prayers from Christians regardless of their spiritual maturity, but many Christians tend to stumble over three common prayer hurdles. (Fred was one of these until he obeyed the call to pray and was motivated by study and mentoring.)

Prayer Hurdle #1—Lack of Consistency

A sporadic prayer life is certainly better than none, but it misses the point of prayer, which is relationship with God.

God is far more interested in a regular, ongoing, and growing relationship with you than He is in your "checking in" once or twice a week or month for an extended length of time. I believe, in other words, that God would prefer ten minutes a day with you in the communion of prayer to communication with you for two hours once a month. Relationship is the focus, and consistency is the key to developing that relationship. Length of time is an important issue in determining the intimacy and depth of a relationship, but consistency must come first. Consistency will lead you naturally to longer periods of time; longer periods of time on a hit-and-miss basis will not lead you toward a consistent pattern of prayer.

Don't let guilt drive you to prayer. That never works, but it is a favorite tactic of the enemy. Any time we pray motivated by guilt, we have lost the heart of the relationship. We do indeed just "check in." When we pray from conviction, however, we pray in an effort to invest in the relationship. Remember that guilt comes from Satan and drives you away from God. Conviction comes from the Holy Spirit and draws you toward God. It seems like a fine line, but there is a big difference. If you have struggled with consistency in your prayer life, remember these three things:

First, there is no condemnation for those who are in Christ Jesus. Through Christ Jesus the law of the Spirit of life sets you free from the law of sin and death (Rom. 8:1). Satan has no hold on you. You belong to Jesus!

Second, God loves you unconditionally. Christianity is not a performance-based religion. It is a relationship based on faith in God through His Son, Jesus Christ (Eph. 2:8). You can't pray so much as to earn heavenly brownie points and you can't pray so little as to end up in the spiritual "doghouse." But the quality of your relationship with God does depend on the amount of time you invest in prayer. Remember, go for consistency first, then longer periods of time will come naturally.

Third, God's heart is grace-oriented. Remember the story of the prodigal son? He left home, wasted his money, lived with bad character, yet his father still took him back with open arms. The same is true with God. No matter how long it's been since you have been consistent in or excited about your prayer life, He will always take you back in an instant with open arms. God is much more interested in your future spiritual growth than He is in your past spiritual shortcomings.

In school I remember my papers being returned to me graded from a negative perspective. A spelling test, for example, might read "–2" or "2 wrong." I believe a better way is to show how many the student got right! The same spelling test, if there were twenty words total, would read "18 correct"— the same results but with a positive and motivating approach. God focuses on how many you get right, Satan focuses on how many you get wrong. The point is, while God does care about our shortcomings, He always operates out of His basic nature, which is love. His love is unconditional, undeserved, and best of all, unending. This truth gives us permission and confidence to move toward God in prayer.

Prayer Hurdle #2—Lack of Listening

Any successful communication in a relationship must be two-way. I'm sure you have known someone who seemed to do all the talking, or more pointedly, never seemed to listen. Relationships that fall into this pattern are doomed to failure or at least produce unhealthy and unproductive results.

If when you pray you do all the talking and almost no listening, there is little opportunity for your relationship with God to develop. It is also difficult to receive direction from God if you spend all of your prayer time explaining the problem rather than listening for the solution. The best prayer times are largely spent with a closed mouth, an open heart, and a pen in hand. I am deeply convinced that the God who created the entire universe, and everyone and everything in it, has something of value to say to us. If we do all the talking, we will never hear what He has to say.

We fear silence. Whether alone or in a group, we get very uncomfortable without noise. The truth is that silence begins to reveal our real self. In silence, we slow down enough to see who we really are in comparison to God, and this makes us uncomfortable. In some of my more mischievous moments I will purposely leave a small prayer group hanging in midair to see how long it takes until someone blurts out something profoundly irrelevant just to break the silence. Afterward, with a good laugh, they confess to bullets of sweat because of their discomfort with silence. An important lesson to learn, whether alone or in a group, is the difference between dead silence and living stillness. The latter of the two is where we meet God.

Practice silence in your prayer. Begin with one-quarter to one-third of your time listening for the voice of God, moving up eventually to one-half of your prayer time. This can be unnerving at first, but don't get discouraged and start talking again. God really does have something to say to you. In time you will learn to discern His voice. In the times of silence when God doesn't speak, just be still and know that He is God.

Prayer Hurdle #3—Lack of Faith

We all lack faith. It's the simple truth. If you and I *really* believed that Jesus could move mountains, heal the sick, and raise the dead, wouldn't we pray more for miracles? Instead, we pray for a good parking spot at the mall, something that requires no faith or trust in God. I intend no sarcasm here, I'm simply commenting on normal Christian behavior (mine included).

Your faith may be based more on what you believe than what God has promised. To reverse this, and believe more on the promises of God than your own finite beliefs, you must stretch your faith by trusting God completely. The good news is that it's not how much faith you have, but whom your faith is in. I can have all the faith in the world that my car will start in the morning, but if the battery is dead, or there is some problem with the engine, I'm not going any- where. Jesus is the Person and the power of your faith. Even on days when you don't feel like praying or you aren't sure

He's listening or will answer, Jesus will make up the difference. Your responsibility is to stretch your faith that day by trusting in the truth and faithfulness of Jesus and praying. If you aren't sure it can happen but believe God can make it happen, you are on the right track.

> Believe me when I say that I am in the Father and the Father is in me; or at least believe on the evidence of the miracles themselves. I tell you the truth, anyone who has faith in me will do what I have been doing. He will do even greater things than these, because I am going to the Father. And I will do whatever you ask in my name, so that the Son may bring glory to the Father. You may ask me for anything in my name, and I will do it (John 14:11–14).

Whatever we ask—in Jesus' name! That means we will receive anything we ask for according to God's will and His ultimate plan. This isn't a mysterious agenda known only by God, Billy Graham, and your pastor. God makes His plan clear in the Bible. Even if you are not sure how to pray, go to God as a child would go to his or her father, and ask. If your motives are pure, there is no wrong prayer. You are surely safe in knowing your motives are pure if you pray for the benefit of another, but praying for yourself is also important. Ask God and then listen. Soon you will learn to pray with more confidence as you see your prayers answered. This process will greatly increase your faith, and you will pray even more. The key is to get started.

Another important point is not to base your faith upon what the answer is. Base it on the fact that Jesus did answer. There are three basic answers to your prayers: "Yes," "No," and "Not now." It's easy to fall into the trap of thinking that if God gives you a yes, then He has answered. "No's" and "not now's" are often misunderstood as nonanswers. He did answer, just not the way you wanted. We all learn more of how to pray by paying attention to how God answers prayer.

ENGAGE IN SPIRITUAL WARFARE

This advanced level of prayer takes the offensive. This kind of prayer initiates a stand against the enemy and his tactics to destroy the church. This is not a "more spiritual" level, but a more advanced level of engagement in prayer that comes with time and experience. We all have the same spiritual status before the Lord, but some have traveled farther in their Christian walk.

Do not engage in this level of prayer until you have first demonstrated a consistent prayer time with God on a one-to-one basis. A good rule of thumb is to realize consistency and enjoy the richness of your growing relationship with God for a full year before taking on the enemy. Think of it as getting in shape before getting into the boxing ring. If you get in too soon, you won't even know what hit you.

Your preparation for spiritual battle begins with putting on your spiritual armor. This armor is found in Ephesians 6:10–18.

Finally, be strong in the Lord and in his mighty power. Put on the full armor of God so that you can take your stand against the devil's schemes. For our struggle is not against flesh and blood, but against the rulers, against the authorities, against the powers of this dark world and against the spiritual forces of evil in the heavenly realms. Therefore put on the full armor of God, so that when the day of evil comes, you may be able to stand your ground, and after you have done everything, to stand. Stand firm then, with the belt of truth buckled around your waist, with the breastplate of righteousness in place, and with your feet fitted with the readiness that comes from the gospel of peace. In addition to all this, take up the shield of faith, with which you can extinguish all the flaming arrows of the evil one. Take the helmet of salvation and the sword of the Spirit, which is the word of God. And pray in the Spirit on all occasions with all kinds of prayers and requests. With this in mind, be alert and always keep on praying for all the saints.

God has fitted us with perfect uniforms for spiritual warfare.

- **Put on the belt of truth.**
  God's truth protects you against Satan's lies.
- **Put on the breastplate of righteousness.**
  Your righteousness in God protects your heart as a believer.
- **Put on the shoes of peace.**
  They protect you from anxiety, confusion, and inner turmoil, and they prepare you for battle.
- **Put on the shield of faith.**
  It protects you from the attacks of temptation.
- **Put on the helmet of salvation.**
  It protects your mind, where spiritual battles are either won or lost.
- **Put on the sword of the Spirit.**
  The only offensive piece is the Word of God. We are to know, speak, and live by the Word of God.

You mentally "put on" each of these pieces just as if you were getting spiritually dressed for battle. Pray through this passage, asking God to gird you in these weapons for warfare. Then you can pray specifically against Satan's top five tactics, which are: to prevent humility through promoting self-sufficiency; to prevent unity through creating division; to prevent commitment through encouraging complacency; to prevent joy through causing discouragement; and to prevent spiritual growth through worldly temptations.

With these five weapons in his arsenal, Satan can do great damage to the church. Praying specifically against the success of these efforts in the name of Jesus will profoundly advance the cause of Christ, and at the same time give the devil one major black eye!

BEGIN A PASTOR'S PRAYER PARTNER MINISTRY

During his years at Skyline, every Sunday morning by 7:30 A.M., you would find John Maxwell's prayer partners in the sanctuary laying hands on the pews, asking God to do a work in the lives of the people that day. (The prayer partner ministry is so important John Maxwell has written an entire book on this topic entitled *Partners in Prayer*.) These partners would touch the pews where people would soon gather, and pray powerful prayers of faith, hope, healing, and love, all in Jesus' name. Doctors and lawyers, craftsmen and laborers, schoolteachers and businesspeople, all side by side with no distinctions before the Lord.

By 8:00 A.M. the partners would huddle together and lay hands on Pastor John and pray God's blessing on him. It didn't stop there; several prayer partners would go to a special room and pray throughout the entire worship service. This happened during all four services. It was so much fun to watch the groupings of prayer partners come out of the upper room with so much enthusiasm they nearly tripped over each other coming down the stairs behind the platform, asking: "Well, what did God do?" They had great expectations after an hour in prayer, and God never let them down.

Nothing will impact the ministry of your church with the magnitude of organized prayer partners. This literally will allow you to tap into the very power of God. Your pastor can work himself into an exhausted heap in the corner of your church if he operates for any length of time without strategic prayer support. His own prayers are vitally important, but not enough. He needs you and many others praying with him for the ministry of your church.

You would never consider pushing your car with the motor off, right? It is only common sense to tap into that horsepower under the hood and use that force to drive the car. Ministry without organized strategic prayer power is like pushing your car to work. You might get there, but even if you do, you won't be good for anything else. You can do ministry without prayer, but not for long and with greatly limited results.

On a trip to Seoul, Korea, to learn firsthand of the power of prayer at the church of Dr. Paul Yonggi Cho, I experienced what would forever change my life and increase my passion for intercession. Our group was invited to an all-night prayer meeting. I thought, *Sounds good. After all, this is why we came.* We had all been in at least one all-night prayer meeting and participated in numerous prayer vigils in the United States. Of course, our idea of an all-night prayer meeting included great conversation, a little teaching, a few catnaps, and vast amounts of coffee strong enough to walk across the sanctuary on its own. This was going to be different, and we had no idea how much! In life's school of prayer I was soon to discover that I was barely in kindergarten.

Standing there with my mouth open, eyes moist, and heart pounding, I had never seen anything like it. Twenty-five thousand people packed into every seat in the auditorium already passionately engaged in prayer before it was time to begin! Hundreds of people stood outside to pray all night because there was no room. We prayed out loud and the sound was like a roar, but totally in order and very organized. Dr. Cho's church knew exactly what they were doing, and they had obviously done this before. You could feel God's presence and power. We left around midnight; they stayed all night.

As I was about to step into the elevator to leave that great church, I turned back for one last look. I wanted to remember that picture of life-changing prayer power in action. There is no doubt in my mind why this church has more than one million members, with seven services on Sunday of twenty-five thousand each—and even at that the people are only allowed to attend approximately once a month. Can you imagine this conversation: "Hello, Pastor. Do you think I could sneak in an extra Sunday this month?"

"Well, Dave, we're not likely to have any cancellations, but if we do, I'll give you a call."

Hundreds of churches today are giving testimony as to the power of prayer in their church. Churches are experiencing rapid growth, people are receiving Christ as Savior, revival is breaking out, and healings are taking place—but only in churches where people have come together to pray.

Steps to Organizing a Prayer Partner Ministry

1. The pastor selects a personal prayer partner.

The partner must have the gift of intercession, be loyal to the pastor, committed to the church, and a mature Christian.

2. The pastor and or board selects a prayer partner team leader.

The qualifications for the leader are the same as in Step 1, with the exception that his primary spiritual gift should be administration. This person functions as the organizer of the prayer partners.

3. Select the rest of the team.

The team of three (the pastor, pastor's intercessor, and the team leader) now select the rest of the team. Invite five more prayer partners to complete the core team. This will provide seven prayer partners, one for every day of the week. Your church can do well with this number for an indefinite period of time, or increase to fourteen, thirty, or more. Don't increase just for numbers' sake, but select people who are truly committed to pray.

4. Recruit prayer partners.

If your pastor desires to increase the number of prayer partners, the recruiting can be done as simply as an announcement from the pulpit, or as elaborately as a prayer partner banquet or retreat. The more personal the approach, the better.

5. Organize your prayer efforts.

The amount of ongoing prayer efforts is limited only to your imagination. The team leader can organize a schedule for prayer partners to pray through every Sunday service, to pray over your pastor before the service, to pray for the whole city for salvation and revival, to pray for the staff, to pray for the ministries of the church, and/or to pray for the offertory every Sunday. If you have a large number of prayer partners, you can select seven captains, one for each day of the week, and organize all the others under the captains.

6. Keep communication open and frequent.

Ongoing communication with the prayer partners is important. A monthly letter should be sent from either the pastor, the pastor's intercessor, or the team leader to keep the prayer partners informed and up-to-date on the events, ministries, and prayer requests of the pastor.

7. Take time away together.

A semiannual or quarterly one-day prayer retreat will add greatly to the sustained vision and encouragement of the prayer partner team. The retreat should include teaching on prayer, vision casting for the church, fellowship and conversation about the ministry of the church, and of course, much prayer.

PRAY STRATEGICALLY FOR THE LIFE AND MINISTRY OF YOUR CHURCH

The results of firing a rifle and a shotgun vary greatly. Both can get the job done, but a rifle shot can travel a much greater distance and has a powerful impact on a specific target. With a shotgun you point and spray, hoping to get a few pellets into the target. With a rifle, you also have the ability to rapidly fire multiple shots.

While shotgun prayers certainly have their place (the most common plea of which is "Lord, help us!" or in real emergencies, "Lord, help us and help us right now!"), rifle prayers have the greater impact. Knowing what you are aiming for, and all firing in the same direction will yield powerful results.

Prayer Essentials

There are seven areas in the church that absolutely require prayer on a regular basis. If you faithfully and consistently pray for the following, your church will recognize powerful blessings.

New visitors.

Pray that God would speak to the hearts of people in your community who do not attend church, and pray that your congregation would reach out and invite new people to church.

People to receive Christ as Savior.

This is listed here not as second in priority to visitors but second in a logical sequence. Without new visitors, there can be no new converts! Pray that God would melt the hearts of those who don't know Him as personal Savior, that they would seek a relationship with Christ. Pray that your church develops a passionate heart for the lost and responds with lifestyle evangelism. My heart has been warmed and motivated by prayer warriors like Diana Ikeler. Diana is a devoted woman of prayer and has a passion for the lost. She has influenced me and other leaders to keep our hearts burning for people who don't know Christ. You can make a difference just as Diana has!

The Holy Spirit's power.

The Spirit of God in us, the Holy Spirit, is the power that brings all the lasting fruit or results in the church. What we can accomplish on our own is extremely limited and short-lived. Pray for God's anointing power to energize your church and truly make an eternal difference.

A spirit of love and unity.

Scripture calls us to both a spirit of love and a spirit of unity. One cannot exist without the other.

> I, therefore, the prisoner of the Lord, beseech you to walk worthy of the calling with which you were called, with all lowliness and gentleness, with longsuffering, bearing with one another in love, endeavoring to keep the unity of the Spirit in the bond of peace. There is one body and one Spirit,

just as you were called in one hope of your calling; one Lord, one faith, one baptism; one God and Father of all, who is above all, and through all, and in you all (Eph. 4:1–6 NKJV).

Pray that your church remains steadfast in its commitment to love one another and actively seeks the unified spirit that pleases the Lord.

Maturing of the body of Christ.

Praying for new people and salvation have been stated already, but what's next? Is God's design salvation alone? No. Philippians 1:6 teaches us that God desires to complete the good work He began in us. So what is this completion? What does it look like?

And He Himself gave some to be apostles, some prophets, some evangelists, and some pastors and teachers, for the equipping of the saints for the work of ministry, for the edifying of the body of Christ, till we all come to the unity of the faith and of the knowledge of the Son of God, to a perfect man, to the measure of the stature of the fullness of Christ; that we should no longer be children, tossed to and fro and carried about with every wind of doctrine, by the trickery of men, in the cunning craftiness of deceitful plotting, but, speaking the truth in love, may grow up in all things into Him who is the head—Christ—from whom the whole body, joined and knit together by what every joint supplies, according to the effective working by which every part does its share, causes growth of the body for the edifying of itself in love (Eph. 4:11–16 NKJV).

God literally calls for us to "grow up" from being children to maturity in our faith. One of the best ways to tangibly measure this maturity is by our servant's heart operating through our God-given gifts in volunteer ministry. Another clear evidence of spiritual maturity is the fruit of the Spirit listed in Galatians 5:22–23 (love, joy, peace, patience, kindness, goodness, faithfulness, gentleness, and self-control). Pray for your congregation to rise up to this level of maturity.

The leadership.

Pray for the primary leaders in your church. The staff, the church board, and the key ministry leaders need your prayer support. Pray that they would be full of wisdom, live with integrity, and always put God's agenda first.

Your pastor.

This relates to the central theme of the book. Here is a weekly prayer plan for your pastor.

HOW TO PRAY FOR YOUR PASTOR

Monday: Pray for your pastor's family.
- God's peace and protection
- A growing love relationship with his wife
- A commitment to quality and quantity time together

Tuesday: Pray for wisdom for your pastor.
- The mind of Christ
- Godly decision making
- Understanding of biblical truth

Wednesday: Pray for your pastor's ministry focus.
- Clear vision
- Commitment to biblical priorities
- Remain true to his God-given gifts and strengths

Thursday: Pray for your pastor's health.
- Protection of his body and mind
- An extra portion of stamina and strength
- Commitment to stress-releasing activity

Friday: Pray for your pastor's spiritual growth.
- A heart for God and the lost
- Fresh biblical insights
- Personal devotions not related to sermon preparation

Saturday: Pray for your pastor's purity.
                 ◆ Pure motives
                 ◆ Pure thought life and faithfulness to his wife
                 ◆ Pure commitment to complete integrity

Sunday: Pray for God's anointing on your pastor.
                 ◆ Strength in his leadership
                 ◆ Passion in his preaching
                 ◆ Fruit and joy in his ministry

You can accomplish this prayer plan in three minutes a day. Of course, you are not limited to three minutes! You can invest as much time as you have. Any number of variations of this plan will work well. For example, instead of praying daily through these topics, you might choose to pray through all of these topics on one particular day each week. This is literally the best gift you can give your pastor. It will not only be incredibly supportive and encouraging, but will also produce dramatic effects.

Tell your pastor you are praying for him. This will lift his spirits and further strengthen his ministry when he knows that specific people are praying for him. You can pray "in secret" and God will certainly honor those prayers. But the human part of your pastor needs to know you are praying. Occasionally send him a note telling him how you prayed for him that day. Pray on!

STEPS TOWARD ACTION

1. Make a personal commitment to firmly establish your own prayer life.
2. Focus on consistency to develop a regular practice of prayer in order to cultivate your relationship with God.
3. Practice silence in your prayer times—God will meet you there. Listen.
4. Remember that guilt drives you away from God and conviction pulls you toward God. His love for you is unconditional.

5. Practice putting on the armor of God found in Ephesians 6.
6. Learn the five tactics Satan uses to destroy the church. Write them down in your Bible.
7. Begin or participate in a pastor's prayer partner ministry.
8. Learn the seven prayer essentials for your church. Write them down inside your Bible.
9. Write down your prayer plan for your pastor inside your Bible.
10. Tell your pastor, or write him a note, about your commitment to a prayer plan for him. Ask if there is anything he would like to add to the list.

"BUT I DON'T WANT TO TEACH THE FOUR-YEAR-OLDS"

"Busy is probably the most commonly used word among our circle of friends," commented Ron and Janene Kraft. "We didn't need one more thing to do . . . until we uncovered the unmatched fulfillment of kingdom service."

Here is Ron and Janene's story:

For us as new Christians, *ministry* was a pretty intimidating word. "What's your ministry?" friends would ask, as traditional images of building projects and baby-burping quickly leaped to mind. Not being overly enthusiastic about either of these possibilities, we knew there must be something else we could do that would be meaningful to us. But was ministry about our need, or God's? The answer surprised us . . . it's about both!

Ron and I are confident that God knows the needs of our church and the gifts He has breathed into us to accomplish them. That confidence comes from watching God use my marketing ability and spiritual gift of leadership to orchestrate outreach events, and Ron's musical talent and spiritual gift of teaching to lead people through worship to the throne of God. But the role we play doesn't stop there. After ten years in ministry it has become our passion to consistently remain intimately aware of our pastor's vision for our church so that we can explore the vast and varied ways we can be of service. We learned that ministry isn't about fitting in. It's about reaching out! Ministry isn't about "doing your time" but expanding God's resources. When Ron and I are caring enough to find the real need, we can be creative enough to do what we can with the gifts we have. God doesn't want us to bide our time in ministry. He wants us to invest our resources—the gifts within that find their highest fulfillment in serving His church.

Ron is a professor of business, an author, and a consultant. Janene is a business owner in the field of marketing. They are the parents of three great boys and a beautiful girl. Ron and Janene are a pastor's delight, but even more important, God's delight, as they endeavor to build His kingdom by serving their church.

THE BIBLICAL FOUNDATION FOR LAY MINISTRY

My wife, Patti, teaches the four-year-olds at Skyline. On Sunday school preparation nights our living room floor looks like a cross between a day-care center and a trade show for mutant puppets. It's amazing what she can do with construction paper, a stapler, and those colorful sprinkles you glue onto every surface imaginable (you know the ones—those little things that resist even a turbo-powered vacuum cleaner).

One Sunday was particularly rough for her. She had twenty-six students, nineteen of them were boys, and there was only one helper. The kids were nearly out of control. The good news was that Patti let them all live. That afternoon I said to her, "You know, Hon, you don't have to do this ministry. There are other ministry opportunities where people don't wet their pants and cry when they don't get their way." Her response was amazing. With tears in her eyes she said, "I love those kids, and God has called me to teach them."

Not everyone responds quite so favorably to children's ministry. Actually, some folks liken it to something between malaria and a root canal. But that's one of the wonderful things about the body of Christ—we're all so different, and by

God's design. God takes that uniqueness and weaves it into His plan for our lives, a plan that always includes making a contribution into others' lives. The most common form of contribution is volunteer ministry in a local church.

Every time I think of the fact that Jesus handed His ministry over to twelve men whom you or I may not have trusted our dirty laundry to, I am amazed. Think about just a few of the crew: rough fishermen, a tax collector, and a revolutionary! I'm even more astonished to realize that God has not changed His plan, and the plan includes me! It also includes you. The idea of servanthood in a local church is not new; God designed it from the beginning and has a place for you to serve in His church. The following reasons will help motivate you to get involved.

THE RIGHT REASONS TO SERVE

Express Gratitude for What Jesus Has Done for You

When you receive a Christmas gift, it's second nature to thank the giver in some way. Expressing gratitude is a natural part of our lives. Ingratitude is an unacceptable trait and often results in damaged relationships. Thankfulness shows appreciation not only for the gift itself, but for the relationship that's behind it.

When you serve as part of your church's volunteer team, you are expressing gratitude for what God has done for you through His Son, Jesus. That's why Christian service is a life-long commitment. Unlike a birthday present from a friend, God's gift lasts for eternity. It's a gift that keeps on living. And God's gift of eternal life is free—you can't earn it, buy it, or work for it. It's free to you because Jesus paid the price for your sin on the cross. He gave His life for your eternal life.

Paul says it clearly in Ephesians 2:8–10: "For it is by grace you have been saved, through faith—and this not from yourselves, it is the gift of God—not by works, so that no one can boast. For we are God's workmanship, created in Christ Jesus to do good works, which God prepared in advance for us to do."

Don't ever take for granted the greatest of all gifts, eternal life with God. Serve with joy and you will be blessed!

God Never Intended for Your Pastor to Do All the Ministry

Seeing the pastor in the pulpit and the people in the pews reminds me of a professional basketball game. There are ten players down on the court, exhausted and in need of a break, and there are twenty thousand spectators eating popcorn and ice cream, in desperate need of exercise.

No matter how good and capable your pastor is, he can't minister to all the needs of the people. If you don't participate in ministry you are forcing someone else (or your pastor) to carry more than God intended. The other possibility is that the specific ministry God intended will not get done. God's plan is for your pastor to equip you to do the ministry. The sign in front of your church could rightly say: Equipper: Rev. Herman U. Ticks. Ministers: The Whole Congregation.

Paul says in Ephesians 4:11–13 (italics mine):

> It was he who gave some to be apostles, some to be prophets, some to be evangelists, and some to be pastors and teachers, to *prepare God's people for works of service,* so that the body of Christ may be built up until we all reach unity in the faith and in the knowledge of the Son of God and become mature, attaining to the whole measure of the fullness of Christ.

Give your pastor permission to equip you for ministry by volunteering for service. "Getting equipped" means being trained and prepared for the ministry you select in your church.

Serve as Part of God's Plan for Church Growth

God intended from the very beginning for His church to grow. Jesus gave us the plan for church growth in Matthew: "All authority in heaven and on earth has been given to me.

Therefore *go and make disciples* of all nations, baptizing them in the name of the Father and of the Son and of the Holy Spirit, and teaching them to obey everything I have commanded you. And surely I am with you always, to the very end of the age" (Matt. 28:18–20, italics mine).

You became part of the church when you received Christ as your personal Savior. Regardless of your church background or denomination, you are part of God's church in the big picture. The church is not made up of four walls, a baptismal, and a foyer. The church is made up of people, God's people.

You also became part of the plan for growth. The bottom line of the Great Commission (Matt. 28:19–20) is "go and make disciples." There are many ways to be part of your church team as together you go about making disciples. What is nonnegotiable is whether or not you are part of the team. You are on the team—congratulations! Now the question is, Will you sit on the sidelines or get in the game? I'm not referring to how much you do, but saying that you must do *something*. It doesn't matter if you serve one hour a month in the nursery or twenty hours a week as a leader in the church. Just get in the game.

As in professional football, no team ever won a game without commitment resulting in successful action toward the mission. In the case of football, the mission is to make more touchdowns than the other team. The mission of the church is making disciples. The "scoreboard" for the church is decisions for Christ. Every time someone receives Jesus as Savior, the scoreboard says: God – 1, Satan – 0. The key question for you is, What are you doing as part of the team to increase the score for God?

To Make a Difference in Life That Will Last for Eternity

I want to make a difference in life, and my hunch is you do too. The fact that you are reading this book tells me something about you. I'm confident you want to avoid the "gold watch syndrome"—doing the same thing for fifty years, getting a gold watch for retirement, and giving up all activity—at all costs. You don't want your whole life to culminate in a little piece of jewelry!

In order to make a difference that breaks out of your personal limitations and extends beyond the boundaries of your abilities, you need to embrace a vision that is bigger than you. Your church's mission or vision is bigger than you; no one person can make it happen. Only through a collective effort of many people can the dreams that really matter come true. There is no better place to see godly dreams come true than in the local church.

As your heart moves in this direction, consider some reasons for which you should *not* serve.

WRONG REASONS TO SERVE

Guilt

The Lord never intended for guilt to be a motivating factor. You are not a second-class citizen or a lazy bum if you are not serving. However, you are definitely missing out on God's plan for you and possibly walking on thin ice over the cold waters of disobedience. Remember the difference between guilt and conviction: Guilt comes from the devil and drives you away from God. Conviction comes from God's Holy Spirit and draws you toward God.

Pressure

"There is no one else to do the job" is the wrong reason to serve in a ministry. First of all, it's not true. I guarantee you that I could find *one* other person in your church to do the job. And second, God created you with a uniqueness that doesn't allow for random placement in ministry. You may need to help out with something in your church that isn't really "you" because your pastor really needs you, but that is temporary. For your long-term ministry, you will want to find the one that most closely fits your spiritual gifts, personality, and desire.

To Please Someone

We are all tempted on occasion to please man instead of God, but Paul wrote in Galatians 1:10: "Am I now trying to win the approval of men, or of God? Or am I trying to please men? If I were still trying to please men, I would not be a servant of Christ." (See also 1 Thess. 2:4.)

Ultimately, the only one to please is God. Surprise—you can also serve to please yourself in that you perform your ministry with such excellence and integrity that you know you gave it your best. Your pastor will be pleased indirectly by your pleasing God!

Pride

Ego can be a healthy strength or the beginning of a downfall. Ego in check can give you a great deal of positive drive and motivation. Ego out of control is guaranteed to cause damage, usually in the area of relationships. Don't volunteer for ministry in positions of power and prestige if you know that pride is an issue for you. Volunteer for an area of pure service until your heart finds joy in the simplicity of service itself.

To Earn Salvation

There is nothing you can do to earn your salvation. It is a free gift from God. The amount of ministry you perform doesn't have a bearing on your spiritual maturity. Your salvation is secure in Christ. Serve in freedom and with joy.

BLESSINGS FROM VOLUNTEER SERVICE

God always gives more than we do. And in the case of service in your church, you will be blessed personally far more than you bless others. Look over the following list of blessings and see if God doesn't give them to you as He has me and so many others.

Your Life Is More Fruitful

You literally become an instrument of changed lives. Your life has impact on others for all eternity. You will have a spiritual productivity that is greater than you could ever experience on your own.

Your Life Is More Fulfilled

When you lay your head down on your pillow at night, you will have a deep and abiding sense that what you are doing is important. You will know that what you're doing truly matters and counts for something significant in the eyes of God.

Your Life Is More Fun

When your life becomes fruitful and fulfilled, you can't help but have some fun! I'm referring more to an inner joy than an outer happiness. Sometimes ministry can be challenging, but joy is your reward.

SPIRITUAL GIFTS

What is a spiritual gift? C. Peter Wagner, professor at Fuller Theological Seminary and church growth consultant, defines it this way: "A spiritual gift is a special attribute given by the Holy Spirit to every member of the Body of Christ according to God's grace for use within the context of the Body."

Spiritual gifts are a special enabling or power for spiritual service that builds up the body of Christ. I believe the "gift" *is* the Holy Spirit; as believers we don't receive just certain parts of the Holy Spirit but all of Him. God then, in His sovereign wisdom, manifests this gift through believers according to the needs of His kingdom.

Four key questions:

♦ Who gives the gifts?	The Holy Spirit.
♦ Who receives the gifts?	Every born-again believer.

♦ Who chooses the gifts?   God, according to His grace.

♦ Where and how are the gifts used?   Within the body, to build up the body.

We read in 1 Peter 4:10: "Each one should use whatever gift he has received to serve others, faithfully administering God's grace in its various forms."

Foundational to this discussion is Paul's teaching on spiritual gifts in Romans 12:4–8:

> Just as each of us has one body with many members, and these members do not all have the same function, so in Christ we who are many form one body, and each member belongs to all the others. We have different gifts, according to the grace given us. If a man's gift is prophesying, let him use it in proportion to his faith. If it is serving, let him serve; if it is teaching, let him teach; if it is encouraging, let him encourage; if it is contributing to the needs of others, let him give generously; if it is leadership, let him govern diligently; if it is showing mercy, let him do it cheerfully.

Another passage referring to spiritual gifts is 1 Corinthians 12:4–11, 27–28:

> There are different kinds of gifts, but the same Spirit. There are different kinds of service, but the same Lord. There are different kinds of working, but the same God works all of them in all men. Now to each one the manifestation of the Spirit is given for the common good. To one there is given through the Spirit the message of wisdom, to another the message of knowledge by means of the same Spirit, to another faith by the same Spirit, to another gifts of healing by that one Spirit, to another miraculous powers, to another prophecy, to another distinguishing between spirits [discernment], to another speaking in different kinds of tongues, and to still another the interpretation of tongues. All these are the work of one and the same Spirit, and he gives them to each one, just as he determines. . . . Now you

are the body of Christ, and each one of you is a part of it. And in the church God has appointed first of all apostles, second prophets, third teachers, then workers of miracles, also those having gifts of healing, those able to help others, those with gifts of administration, and those speaking in different kinds of tongues.

It is obvious that there are many kinds of gifts and yet they are all to be used as part of one body, the body of Christ, for the common good of one another. It is important to note that 1 Corinthians 13 emphasizes the superiority of love over all the gifts. Seek love as the "most excellent way" and be sincere in your love for others. Paul wants to make sure we don't get caught in any kind of "gifts competition."

In 1 Corinthians 13 Paul says that you can have all the most wonderful and powerful gifts imaginable, but if you do not have love, you have nothing. There is to be no rank ordering of the gifts. You are neither more nor less spiritual because of the gifts God has chosen to give you. Bruce Fleisher, a good friend of mine and a devoted churchman, has the spiritual gift of "helps" (among others). When he was a young Christian, Bruce once said, "I *just* have the gift of helps." The truth of the matter is that in God's economy, if spiritual gifts were ranked, helps would be toward the top because of the spiritual maturity the gift requires. The gift of helps usually places you in a ministry that doesn't give you much limelight or special recognition. The gift of helps usually has you serving someone, or helping someone else accomplish his or her ministry. It calls for a humble heart, personal security, and a servant's spirit, all of which Bruce consistently demonstrates with a cheerful and mature attitude.

God created and endowed every Christian with spiritual gifts, and He did so with a purpose in mind. Your understanding of this fivefold purpose will help you maximize the potential of your church. Each gift's purpose is to: bring glory to God, strengthen the body of believers, establish unity within the church, bring maturity and personal growth to individual believers, and benefit everyone in the church.

Why You Should Know Your Spiritual Gifts and Use Them

Their fivefold purpose helps you see the big picture of spiritual gifts, and these next three reasons will help you make a more personal connection with your contribution to the body of Christ.

To help you more fully understand God's will for your life.

God has created you unique. There is no one like you in all the world. Your uniqueness, however, is not random. God has created you with a mission in mind. Your spiritual gifts are a significant guiding factor in discovering and understanding God's will for your life.

You are needed to help build the body of Christ.

My kids love to put puzzles together. They have learned that if even one piece is missing the puzzle can't be completed, and the partial construction is more difficult. The body of Christ is the same way; if even one person is missing, the picture is not complete. Some particular function in the body of Christ may not be accomplished without your help and your gifts.

To find more fulfillment and joy in life.

A large percentage of Americans in the workforce today freely admit that they don't like their jobs and would change in a minute if they could. Why? They are not in the right spot. They are not making a significant contribution to anything that matters; therefore, they find little fulfillment and joy. For you as a Christian, fulfillment and joy come from a deep connection to God and His plan for your life. You will notice a dramatic lift in your spirit and motivation in life as you tap more fully into your God-given gifts and participate in the building of your church.

Discover and Use Your Gifts

Anything in life of any substantial value requires some investment on your part. The same is true with discovering your spiritual gifts. This investment, however, will come back to you tenfold. For a relatively small commitment on your part, you can know and use your gifts.

1. Take a spiritual gifts test.

Contact your pastor about taking a spiritual gifts discovery test to help you identify your gift. Don't be nervous; it isn't really a test! It's not something to measure your Bible knowledge. There are no right or wrong answers. The test asks questions about your interests, experience, and preferences as they relate to the body of Christ in the local church. It usually takes about thirty minutes, and it's fun!

Take some time to learn more about spiritual gifts. Ask your pastor if he has any sermon tapes or book recommendations on spiritual gifts. Read the full passages of Scripture in Romans 12, 1 Corinthians 12, and Ephesians 4 as they relate to spiritual gifts.

2. Try out different gifts and ministries.

Remember that the study of spiritual gifts is not an exact science. Don't be rigid in your application of gifts to ministries. Don't box yourself or others into certain ministries because of a certain gift. Use the gifts God has given you first for the benefit of others in your church, and second for your own fulfillment and joy.

If you are not certain about your gifts even after a test, try some on for size. Don't try to put on a gift that you have no hint of possessing or simply because you want a particular gift. God decides what gift you receive. After you have narrowed the list down to several possibilities, experiment with a few in the corresponding ministries in your church and watch for the results. Your pastor or another leader in your church can help match your gifts with the ministry opportunities available.

3. Evaluate your effectiveness.

It is not out of order to expect your spiritual gift to "work." God gave you a gift because He wants you to accomplish something for Him. Desiring to be successful with your spiritual gift(s) does not contradict sincere Christian humility. "When true gifts are in operation, whatever is supposed to happen will happen," writes C. Peter Wagner in his book *Your Spiritual Gifts Can Help Your Church Grow.*[1]

Do you remember the old commercial with a scrappy little old lady who asked: "Where's the beef?" Well, in this case the question is, "Where's the fruit?" Where is the evidence of lives impacted in a positive way as a result of your gifts? Look around you and see what lives have been changed, who has been helped and encouraged, and how your church has benefited because of your gifts.

If the fruit isn't obvious, don't be discouraged, but do take action. You may be in the wrong ministry or you may be focusing on a gift other than the one(s) God has in mind just for you. Just try something else. When you hit the right combination of gifts and ministries, you will know!

4. Look for confirmation from others in your church.

In addition to expecting fruit from your ministry, you can anticipate confirmation to come from the leaders and others in your church. If people are thanking and complimenting you for "a job well done" as a result of your ministry efforts, you are on the right track! On the other hand, be open and receptive particularly to your pastor and other leaders if they feel you may need to try a different ministry. Remember, there is no such thing as the wrong person for a ministry, only the wrong ministry for a person.

Let me close this section with a great quote from Pastor John MacArthur: "No local congregation will be what it should be, what Jesus prayed that it would be, what the Holy Spirit gifted it and empowered it to be, until it understands [and puts into action] spiritual gifts."

TAP INTO YOUR SPIRITUAL PASSION

I no longer qualify for a "bad hair day," but occasionally I have a "bad computer day." At times I'm convinced my computer is possessed. Fortunately, help isn't far away. The INJOY Computer SWAT Team will come in to cast the demons out of my PC. Candidly, I'm not very proficient with anything that has lights, switches, or is remotely mechanical. I personally would love to drive a disposable car.

In contrast, Lonnie Brugman, a faithful servant at Skyline Church, loves technical things—the more buttons the better. At church I could always find Lonnie behind a sound board. He has a passion for mixing sound, recording, and making everyone else look good in the worship service. Lonnie will be the first person to arrive at church to set up a *Star Wars*–like console and the last one to leave after he tears it all down again. He has invested countless hours in this ministry. Why does Lonnie do all of this? It's his passion—both the technical side and helping people.

Your passions, interests, and desires must be an important part of your ministry selection. A longtime friend of mine, Phil Taylor, has a passion for contemporary social issues such as abortion, pornography, and Christianity in public schools. He asked me how he could plug his passion into ministry. At that time there was no organized social concerns ministry at Skyline. Phil volunteered to start one and Concerned Citizens was born. Wonderful, life-changing ministry has taken place because Phil connected his interests and passion with ministry.

Ben could cook—I mean, *really* cook. He was at one time a White House chef, and then God called him to be a chef in His house. Ben loved to do it, and he could feed hundreds of people food that was delicious. I was often organizing the event he was cooking for, so I was rarely seated at a table. As I flew through the kitchen, there Ben would be, holding out a plateful of food, a big smile, and a fork. There was something about his expression that said, "Eat it or wear it." He took his cooking seriously! He would stay for hours to wash dishes and clean up. His reward? On this side of heaven, only a "Thanks, Ben." But that wasn't his motivation. He loved his ministry, and so did we!

There are two sides to passion, one is love and one is hate. You may someday find yourself in a ministry you have a passion to get out of. Charlie Wetzel, John Maxwell's head writer and researcher, had been at Skyline for only two months but he was hungry for ministry. The small group he was attending at the time asked for volunteers for the nursing home ministry and Charlie signed up. It wasn't long before he discovered how ill-suited he was for it. There was nothing about this ministry he liked. He had compassion for the elderly and wanted to serve, but it got so bad he would break out in a cold sweat on the way to the nursing home. He fulfilled the briefest possible commitment and escaped. Charlie is a positive thinker, and if you asked him about his experience, he would only twitch a little and say he did learn something from it—which ministry was not for him!

Since Charlie is a committed churchman, he immediately tried some other ministries, many of which he enjoyed, and realized significant fruit. The ministry that fits his gifts and passion best is as a lay pastor of a small group of believers. This incorporates his gift and passion for teaching as well as leading believers in their process of maturity. Charlie experienced several ministries before he found the one just right for him, but it was worth it. He and his wife, Stephanie, are lay pastors together and both love it.

What can we learn from Charlie's story? First, that it's okay to experiment with different ministries, even if you feel as though you failed at one. Second, it's important to quickly get reinvolved in another ministry. And third, God will come through with a ministry that is just right for you.

What are your passions, interests, and desires in life? What motivates you? What would you do without pay just because you love doing it? The answers to these questions will lead you to the ministry that is just right for you.

INCORPORATE YOUR UNIQUE PERSONALITY

Another piece of the puzzle in the discovery of your ministry is your own personality. Try these questions to get a feel for it:

- **Are you outgoing and talkative, or are you quiet and reserved?**
- **Would you rather work on a short-term project or a long-term relational ministry?**
- **Are you an up-front kind of person or a behind-the-scenes kind of person?**
- **Do you have tremendous amounts of energy or do you run out of gas fairly quickly?**
- **Are you more creative or more analytical?**

Your answers will give your pastor or another leader in your church great insight into the ministry in which you would be most effective.

There are many personality tests available today. One of the most widely used is the Personality Profile made popular by Florence Littauer. Her book, *Personality Plus,* is a delightfully entertaining and very insightful source for an in-depth study.

As we discussed in Chapter 2, the four basic temperaments are Choleric, Sanguine, Phlegmatic, and Melancholy. We will look at these in more detail here. There are positive and negative characteristics of all four types, but each one has a primary thrust. And no person displays only one temperament.

The Choleric is a powerful person who prefers control. A Choleric's strengths include his being a born leader, goal-oriented, decisive, a big-picture visionary, and a self-starter. A Choleric's weaknesses include his being bossy, impatient, too independent or a user, and stubborn. The Sanguine is a popular person who prefers fun. The sanguine person is appealing, talkative, enthusiastic, cheerful, and friendly. A Sanguine's weaknesses include his being a compulsive talker, shallow, self-absorbed, desirous of attention, forgetful, and poor in follow-through. The Phlegmatic is a peaceful person and prefers life on a more easygoing basis. Phlegmatics are easy to get along with, competent and steady, loyal, balanced, thoughtful, and cool under pressure. Phlegmatics can also be unenthusiastic, fearful or worried, stubborn, indecisive, and unmotivated. The Melancholy is a perfectionistic person who may also be a deep thinker, intelligent, detail conscious, a problem solver, sensitive, and creative. A Melancholy's weaknesses include his seeing the negative, being moody, not people-oriented, too introspective, and over-exacting.

You can probably see a little of yourself in all the personalities, but you are dominant in only one type, and usually display a secondary type.

So how does all this work? If you are a strong Melancholy, for example, you probably do not want to be on the hospitality committee. A Sanguine, however, might thrive in that ministry. A Phlegmatic may feel uncomfortable in a high-pressure decision-making or recruiting board position, while a Choleric might excel in the same ministry. A Melancholy might do very well in a detailed follow-up program, but that would drive a Choleric crazy. I've purposely given only a brief sketch of the connection between personality and ministry because it's not wise to put this into a formula. You will know in your heart if a ministry fits you or not. The greatest value in taking the Personality Profile is to help you relate better to others in whatever ministry you select.

TAKE THE INITIATIVE

Don't wait for your pastor or another leader in your church to ask you to get involved in a ministry. Jump in, go for it! You aren't locked in for life; if you try a ministry that's not right for you, you can try another. You can even pioneer your own ministry if your church doesn't have one that seems to be designed for you. The most important thing is to get involved. Support your pastor, please God, and build your church!

─STEPS TOWARD ACTION─

1. Give your pastor "permission" to be the equipper in your church.
2. Don't expect your pastor to perform all the ministry in your church; part of the ministry is your job.
3. Make a sound commitment to participate in the growth of your church.
4. Ask God how you can make the greatest impact for His kingdom.
5. Review the wrong reasons to serve and check your own heart according to that list.
6. Discover your spiritual gifts.
7. Make sure you focus on love over any of the gifts.
8. Make a connection between your passion and your ministry.
9. Make sure your personality fits your ministry.
10. Get in the game!

GOD LOVES A CHEERFUL GIVER

"We thought we had our spiritual bases covered by attending Sunday school, church, and helping in ministries. It wasn't until God took us through a growth process in which we developed humble and grateful hearts that we realized what being good stewards really meant," John and Liz Austel shared with me.

Here is John and Liz's story:

We listened to a great sermon on stewardship. In our past experience we only heard about stewardship as it related to money matters. This time, tithing was mentioned, but it was different. It included all aspects of stewardship. The pastor said that stewardship included our gifts, energy, time, and . . . money. We had lunch with a close friend from church to talk about the sermon. We talked about feeling that we were in control of our finances, which in turn brought security to our household. This security was totally rocked, however, when our business suffered a severe blow and we nearly lost everything. We felt helpless. Our humanly manufactured security was gone, which helped us gain a new and right perspective of where our true security is to be based.

We felt so humbled. The Lord had given us so much, and it was obvious He was the only one who could provide for our needs. We asked ourselves a tough question: If we truly love our heavenly Father and are obedient to His Word, how could we possibly justify not returning a portion of what He has entrusted to us?

We began tithing a full 10 percent and making it the first check we wrote each month. It took a couple of months to adjust to our new budget, but we knew it was the right thing to do. God immediately blessed us with a peace and security we had never before known.

We'd like to say that when we finally became consistent tithers, God blessed us financially, and we now have more money than we ever imagined. Actually, we would *love* to be able to say that! The simple truth is, however, that tithing isn't about money. Since we've settled that issue in our life God has blessed our family in ways we cannot begin to name. None of these ways are financial, and we would not trade one of them for all the money on earth.

John and Liz Austel own an insurance business and have committed the stewardship of their company totally to the Lord. They have three high-energy boys and are very dedicated to serving God in their local church.

SETTLE THE LORDSHIP ISSUE

You have to put your shoes on before you can tie the laces—that's just the way things are. My kids try it the other way around, but no matter how much they push, squirm, or wiggle, it doesn't work. They must put the shoe on first, then they can lace it up tight.

There are many things in life that happen only in a certain order. Your commitment to God with your finances is one of those things. Martin Luther said, "There are three conversions: the heart, the mind, and the purse." This is not a reflection of Luther's theology as much as it is his understanding of human behavior. We first give our heart to Jesus, then as we mature we begin to obey, and the last area of full obedience is in the area of our financial faithfulness. Rare is the person who receives Jesus as Savior one day and is tithing 10 percent the next day. Christian stewardship is a process of maturity, trust, and obedience. For some this process is short, for others it takes longer, and unfortunately, for a few it never happens.

Billy Graham said, "If a person gets his attitude toward money straight, it will help him straighten out almost every other area of his life." From Luther to Graham, Christian leaders have known the significance of money in our lives. God knows too. In the Bible there are approximately five hundred verses on prayer, less than that on faith, and more than two thousand verses on money and possessions! Sixteen of the thirty-eight parables deal with money and possessions.

I want to tell you my experience with this area. It was on Easter of 1973 that I received Christ as my Savior. It was an outdoor service with Pastor Orval Butcher preaching in the Mt. Miguel football stadium in Spring Valley, California. God used three words painted on a large backdrop behind the choir to reveal His saving grace to me that morning. Amid the lilies and the blue sky of the backdrop were the words "He Is Risen!" God, in His infinite grace and mercy, made those words come alive in my heart that morning. I couldn't escape them, they were all I could see or think about. God truly spoke to me that day and I knew it was true—He *is* risen!

It seemed as though I had bolted out of the blocks as I began my race of Christian maturity, except in one area: money. My attitude was so bad that every time Pastor Butcher brought up the topic of money, I would become visibly unsupportive by crossing my arms and even rolling my eyes. I decided I would make an appointment and talk to him about the whole thing. We met and I explained how he was making "everybody" feel guilty about "this money thing."

Very lovingly (he was unbelievably patient with me), he asked who "everybody" was.

I stammered and stuttered only to say something like, "Well, that's not the point, that's just how people feel!"

Pastor Butcher then said, "Tell me how *you* feel."

I admitted I felt bad.

He asked if I wanted to know why I felt bad, and I said yes. He looked me in the eyes and spoke the truth in love: "Dan, you feel bad because you are sinning."

My heart sank as God revealed to me that Pastor Butcher was right. Pastor Butcher didn't make me feel miserable—my discomfort came from the Holy Spirit bringing me under conviction. It wasn't my money, it was God's money, and I was simply the steward or manager of it. I would like to tell you that the issue was settled, but the money issue didn't get settled until I settled who was truly Lord of my life.

Jesus said: "No one can serve two masters; for either he will hate the one and love the other, or else he will be loyal to the one and despise the other. You cannot serve God and mammon [money]" (Matt. 6:24 NKJV).

Have you settled the lordship issue? Who is Lord of your life? Is Jesus your Savior or your Savior and Lord? There is a difference. As your Savior, He has unconditionally paid the price for your eternal life. As Savior and Lord, He has not only forgiven your sins but you have declared that there is nothing in your life that comes before Him. Does this imply you are perfect? Absolutely not, we are all growing in grace and never "arrive" at a point of total spiritual maturity this side of heaven. But you can commit to God that there will be no more part-time Christianity. God gave all of Himself to you. Settling the lordship issue means you have made a commitment to give all of yourself to God.

GOD'S EXAMPLE OF GIVING

God doesn't ask us to do anything that He himself didn't do, especially in the area of giving. He is such a wonderful God that He doesn't just bark out orders for us to follow, but shows us the way.

God Gives First

God has always given first. From creation itself to His Son, Jesus, God is a giving God. Scripture says that God is a loving

Father who cares for us and wants the best for us. He has given you time, life itself, talent, treasures, friends, family, peace of mind, love, hope, and eternal life. And that's the short list!

God Gives More

You can't outgive God. Like the old farmer said, "God has a bigger shovel." It's true—you could try to fill the barn with hay all day, and God with one stroke would have the job done. None of us are to give with the hope of getting back, that's the wrong motive. In fact, God doesn't give back, He gives first! We are the ones giving back! I challenge you to try to outgive God You can't do it!

God Gives Unconditionally

God doesn't give with strings attached. He doesn't give like Santa Claus, only if you've been nice, not naughty. The Bible says we've all been naughty with no hope of being nice without Jesus. God gives because it is His nature. He is a loving and generous God.

I was waiting to board a plane at Lindbergh Field in San Diego when I was approached by a Hare Krishna believer. His head was shaved, and he was dressed in a long, flowing, orange robe and sandals. He said to me, "God is love," and handed me a flower. Then he asked for a donation. I didn't give him one, and his response surprised me. He immediately snatched the flower from my hand and went on to the next person! God never takes the flowers back.

TEN REASONS TO BE FAITHFUL IN YOUR TITHE

God has never had a bad idea. Yet some Christians seem to resist very basic parts of Christian living. The following ten reasons will help clarify for you a strong biblical picture of why you need to tithe.

1. God Is Pleased by Your Obedience

Malachi 3:10 says: "'Bring the whole tithe into the storehouse, that there may be food in my house. Test me in this, says the LORD Almighty, 'and see if I will not throw open the floodgates of heaven and pour out so much blessing that you will not have room enough for it.'"

Tithe means a tenth. God has directed us to return only 10 percent of all He has given us to the storehouse (the church). God lets you keep 90 percent, and that's better than the government! I have often been asked if we are to tithe on our gross or our net. My answer is: "Do you want God to bless you on your gross or your net?" There is no rule or Scripture on this, except to say that God does call us to be generous. I believe there is grace in this matter, but remember, you can't outgive God.

In Malachi 3:9, God actually says you are robbing Him if you don't tithe. Remember that God is a God of grace. He chooses to forgive you of everything in your past, so you can begin today with a clean slate.

2. God Is Honored by Your Faithfulness

Proverbs 3:9 says: "Honor the LORD with your wealth, with the firstfruits of all your crops." *Firstfruits* refers to giving to God off the top, not from the leftovers. He gets the first piece of pie, not the crumbs scraped up from the bottom. *Honor* means to hold in high regard, in high esteem, to value. We communicate how much we value, love, and trust God by our tithe.

3. Tithing Helps Keep Your Priorities Straight

In Matthew 6:21 Jesus said, "For where your treasure is, there your heart will be also." This verse can be said both ways with the same meaning. For where your heart is, there also will you lay up your treasures. Jesus is saying that our hearts are easy to read. He knows that our priorities will be revealed by looking at where we store up our treasures. To be very candid with you, your checkbook will give you great insight into your real priorities. Tithing is a tangible way to help you keep your priorities in the right order. A train needs the track to keep going in the right direction and prevent disaster, and we need obedience to the Lord.

4. Tithing Means You Are Eligible for a Blessing

Look back again at Malachi 3:10. God talks about blessing us so much that we won't have room for it! It's important to remember two things about this blessing: First, God *will* bless, and second, God doesn't say *how* He will bless. I do not agree with prosperity theology. God never promised us three Mercedes vehicles in our garage. He never even promised us a garage! But He has promised to meet all our needs, not all our wants. God's blessings come in so many different forms; friends, health, a good marriage, and life itself are just a few. How has God blessed you?

5. Tithing Guards You from Selfishness

Paul wrote in Acts 20:35, "In everything I did, I showed you that by this kind of hard work we must help the weak, remembering the words the Lord Jesus himself said: 'It is more blessed to give than to receive.'" My son, John-Peter, and I were at McDonald's one afternoon when he was nearly four. He was having the all-American meal: burger, cola, and fries while I stared at my boring salad with the dressing on the side. My discipline gave out and I asked John-Peter for a couple of his fries. He said, "No!" I was amazed! After all, didn't he realize where all his food comes from in the first place? How ungrateful, how bold and selfish! Then it struck me—so many people are the same way toward God. We all are, at times. God asks for so little in return for all He gives, and the answer is "No." As for my son, he wasn't yet four; he will grow and mature. The challenge is now for you to examine your heart in this area of giving.

6. God Loves a Cheerful Giver

Paul also instructed us in 2 Corinthians 9:6–11:

Remember this: Whoever sows sparingly will also reap sparingly, and whoever sows generously will also reap

generously. Each man should give what he has decided in his heart to give, not reluctantly or under compulsion, for God loves a cheerful giver. And God is able to make all grace abound to you, so that in all things at all times, having all that you need, you will abound in every good work. As it is written: "He has scattered abroad his gifts to the poor; his righteousness endures forever." Now he who supplies seed to the sower and bread for food will also supply and increase your store of seed and will enlarge the harvest of your righteousness. You will be made rich in every way so that you can be generous on every occasion, and through us your generosity will result in thanksgiving to God.

God wants the best in life for you. He knows the good that will come to you if you tithe. God does want you to give cheerfully. That may not be the way you begin, and that's okay. You may begin with fear, anxiety, or even resentment. These feelings will pass as you begin to mature in your trust in God for your finances. The goal is to progress toward a time when you give with a cheerful heart. Your giving will move beyond sheer obedience to a joyful act of worship.

7. Tithing Supports Your Local Church

In 2 Corinthians 8:2–5 Paul wrote:

Out of the most severe trial, their overflowing joy and their extreme poverty welled up in rich generosity. For I testify that they gave as much as they were able, and even beyond their ability. Entirely on their own, they urgently pleaded with us for the privilege of sharing in this service to the saints. And they did not do as we expected, but they gave themselves first to the Lord and then to us in keeping with God's will.

This is a powerful passage of God's people providing for His church. Supporting your local church encompasses many facets, from the basics like the light bill and the mortgage to the weightier issues of the pastor's salary and fulfilling the Great Commission. However you slice it, the church can't operate without financial backing. For every person who doesn't tithe, another must tithe double or ministry will not happen.

8. Tithing Ensures That Your Needs Will Be Met

Jesus said: "But seek first his kingdom and his righteousness, and all these things will be given to you as well." The passage of Scripture in Matthew 6:25–33 addresses the issue of God meeting our needs. Jesus uses examples such as birds and flowers to illustrate His love for us and His commitment to our provision. Obviously we mean more to God than birds and flowers, yet God cares completely for them. How much more will He care for us?

As I have stated, God has promised to meet all your needs, not all your wants. The sticky issue, then, is your definition of "needs," which is very subjective. Read God's perspective to remove some of the subjectivity. For example, 1 Timothy 6:8 says: "But if we have food and clothing, we will be content with that." God defines our material needs as much more basic than we do. This perspective is helpful in changing our thinking about how much we need. There is nothing wrong with wanting something, and telling God about that desire. It's when you begin to expect more, or believe you deserve more, that a problem arises.

9. Tithing Helps Meet the Needs of God's People

Paul said in his letter to the Corinthians, "Now about the collection for God's people: Do what I told the Galatian churches to do. On the first day of every week, each one of you should set aside a sum of money in keeping with his income, saving it up, so that when I come no collections will have to be made" (1 Cor. 16:1–2). God ministers through you to others by means of your giving. Winston Churchill said, "We make a living by what we get, but we make a life by what we give."

10. Tithing Reminds Us That God Is the True Owner and Giver of All That We Have

We're instructed in 1 Timothy 6:17–18: "Command those who are rich [any one with more than food and clothing] in this present world not to be arrogant nor to put their hope in wealth, which is so uncertain, but to put their hope in God, who richly provides us with everything for our enjoyment. Command them to do good, to be rich in good deeds, and to be generous and willing to share." God created it all, He owns it all, and yet He shares it all. God's expectation is that you will follow His example in giving.

I would like to ask you a personal question. Can you think of a good reason not to tithe? "Can't afford to" doesn't qualify. Ten percent is 10 percent, whether of ten thousand dollars or of fifty million dollars. Why not begin trusting God today? Will you begin tithing?

THE 10–10–80 PLAN

Most people look at budgeting as a nervous breakdown on paper. It doesn't have to be that way. It all depends on how detailed and accurate you want to be. You can purchase computer software that will keep track of more than you want to know, and there are simple notebooks to record the basics.

Over the course of one year, many Americans spend a little more than they make. How is this possible? Credit cards! The magic of plastic makes for happy moments in the present and compounds misery in the future. A friend once said to me, "Want to make a million dollars? Spend less than you make and do it for a long, long time." There is more truth here than meets the eye. The problem is, most people want more than they have and they want it now. How much more? Just a little, but always *more*.

If you have found yourself in the position of debt, there are only two options to get out. You either make more money or spend less money. There is no other way. It's not easy, but it is that simple. It's like dieting (another popular subject); the formula is simple, doing it is difficult. If you consume more calories than you burn, you gain weight. If you burn more calories than you consume, you lose weight. That's it. No fancy diet will ever change that bottom-line reality.

The 10–10–80 Plan is a proven tool to keep you on track. You give God 10 percent of your income, you save 10 percent, and you live on 80 percent. The most common response is, "I couldn't possibly live on only 80 percent of my income." If that is true then you are probably living above your means. If it takes more than 80 percent of your income to pay for everything except tithe and savings, then the answer is to either spend less or make more so you can live on 80 percent. If you are not in debt, this simple plan is enough for you to build a solid financial foundation conservatively and biblically. If you are in debt, this plan is not enough. I recommend that you seek counsel from a Christian financial adviser to design a specific plan to retire the debt before the debt retires you. (Additional help may be found in books written by Christian finance experts such as Larry Burkett and Ron Blue.)

INVESTING WITH ETERNAL VALUE

There are many things in life that are enjoyable, but few that will last. We're a two-car family, and my wife's fourteen-year-old Volvo is terminally ill. Every time she gets in, two thoughts go through her mind: *Will it start? Will it keep going?* We're just a short time or one more tow away from replacing the "yellow monster." It kills me to think about the total investment in that car only to realize that ultimately it's a hunk of metal that will be smashed and tossed into a junkyard.

I was driving by a favorite restaurant we have eaten at countless times. For at least twenty years this restaurant served thousands of people, hundreds of whom were from the church. On a Sunday afternoon, it was like another worship service. The buzz of fellowship was like a choir, at every table there was at least one preacher, and at the end of the meal an offering was taken! Wonderful memories were part of this place, which caused my mouth to drop open as I saw a huge crane swing a wrecking ball right into the side of the building. With a deafening noise it left "my" booth in rubble and dust. It hit me how temporary things in this world really are.

There is nothing wrong with the material things of life, some of which we truly need. But it's important to remember that they will not last. In contrast, every dollar you give to your church will last forever. The worst financial decision of a church will have a greater return than the best financial decision in corporate America.

This isn't a pie-in-the-sky topic. The impact is real and immediate upon you and your family. The money you invest in your church (God's economy), will have a direct impact on your spiritual growth and your children's future. The money you invest in your church will have a direct impact on the spiritual awakening of America. It's up to the church to turn the country around, and that means it's up to you and me. Put your money where it's going to make a difference.

Several years ago at Skyline Church we launched a missions project, sending vans to India to show the film *Jesus*. It was estimated that one van and two films would reach more than one hundred thousand Indians before the van literally fell apart. Few people in our congregation could write out a check for fifteen thousand dollars, the cost of one van, but by drawing together in a unified force we raised enough to send four vans to India. The potential impact for all eternity is nearly unlimited. I don't know how many thousands came to Christ, but I know that every dollar was well spent with eternal results. Long after the vans are gone, people will tell the life-changing story of Jesus Christ, and souls will inherit eternal life.

PROSPERITY THEOLOGY OR FREEDOM FOR MINISTRY?

There was a time when pastors were paid with chickens, a sack of potatoes, and all the hand-me-down clothes they could wear. Those days are gone, and they should be. We read in 1 Timothy 5:17–18: "The elders who direct the affairs of the church well are worthy of double honor, especially those whose work is preaching and teaching. For the Scripture says, 'Do not muzzle the ox while it is treading out the grain,' and 'The worker deserves his wages.'"

Too many church boards have adopted the saying (as it relates to their pastor's salary), "God, you keep him humble and we'll keep him poor." There is nothing spiritual about being poor, just as there is nothing spiritual about being rich. Spirituality is an issue of the heart, not the wallet. I know wealthy people who are deeply committed to God and poor people who barely attend church.

You may not feel that you are in a position to influence your pastor's salary, but you are. I don't recommend that you push to know what the salary is any more than the pastor pushes to know what your salary is. You can, however, talk to someone on the finance board to receive assurance that they are taking good financial care of the pastor and his family.

My goal is not to make every pastor wealthy. This is not "pastoral prosperity theology." Pastors need to be paid well so they can focus on their ministry. If a pastor must worry about how to pay bills and take care of the basics, he can't concentrate on God's business.

When John Maxwell took his first church in Hillham, Indiana, he was paid about eighty dollars a week. Even in 1969, eighty dollars didn't go very far. The church gave John permission to work a job on the side. His wife, Margaret, jumped in and said, "No. My husband is called to serve the Lord full-time and build a great work for Him. I will work instead." And work she did, three jobs to provide the needed income.

Margaret was willing and never complained, and working was her choice, but it should never be the expectation of the church that the pastor's wife work outside the home. The vast majority of churches are able to increase the pastor's salary. If for your church it is a budget issue, what would happen if everyone in the church tithed? (Then it becomes a spiritual issue.)

Think of your pastor as an executive when it comes to setting his salary. That is exactly what he is. He is the chief executive officer of a not-for-profit corporation with responsibility for the bottom line. Even the smallest of churches would carry at least the responsibilities of a small business owner plus the spiritual welfare of all the people! The larger the church and the larger the staff, the more the pastor functions with all the responsibility of a corporate executive, again, with the added dimension of people's spiritual lives.

Make sure that his salary package includes excellent medical and dental coverage, continuing education expenses, a retirement program, self-employment tax compensation, and a meal and car allowance so that when he takes you to lunch he can buy! This is *on top of* his salary. You might ask, "Can we afford all that?" Let me be blunt with you and say that you will reap the fruit of the seeds you sow—little investment, little return. Let's say your church is averaging 180 per Sunday in attendance and the paid staff consists of your pastor and a secretary. It is time to hire an assistant pastor, but you feel there isn't enough money. By not accepting the challenge and stretching the budget, you can literally prevent church growth.

I'm saying "you" but I don't mean you personally (unless you are the head of the finance board). You as an individual can speak up and be supportive of paying your pastor well.

Your pastor isn't in his position to get rich, he's there to serve God, but that doesn't mean he has to be financially punished for doing God's work. I say, reward the pastor, he has one tough job!

The reason I'm so passionate about this issue is because there seems to be a double standard when it comes to the salary a pastor receives. My observation of pastors across the country is that they take criticism if they purchase some of the same things people in the congregation purchase. While the church members are rejoicing about their newly acquired treasures, the pastor takes heat for the same thing.

David was a pastor in a large church who drove a small, nondescript car for years. Nothing was ever said about his car. One day he pulled into the church in a beautiful Cadillac. You would have thought he'd stolen the car at gunpoint. David had always been considered a spiritual man of God, yet many now wondered if he had gone the way of the world. The talk was rampant. The irony is that some of the strongest criticism came from people who drove nicer and more expensive cars!

The fact was that the Cadillac was five years old and had been given to him as a gift. Even if this had not been the case, David should have been able to drive the car he wanted to if it fit within reasonable patterns of stewardship.

Another pastor friend and his wife had saved their money for twenty years to go on a cruise for their twentieth anniversary. They scrimped and saved every nickel in anticipation for the trip of a lifetime. They had so much fun planning the cruise during their eighteenth and nineteenth years, they could hardly wait to go. When they told their church family about the dream celebration, the pastor nearly lost his job. The congregation was small and very conservative. They couldn't understand why the pastor, a spiritual man, would put so much value in such an extravagant celebration. The clergy couple were deeply hurt and robbed of much of the joy of their dream anniversary trip.

Another pastor friend of mine put a swimming pool in his backyard. The church was in a relocation building program at the time and many people severely criticized his decision. The pastoral couple were treated as if they were not truly committed to the project. A large number of people in the church ignored the facts that his spouse had a well-paying job and her parents chose to help with the pool as a gift to their grandkids. The interesting thing was that two of the largest objectors had swimming pools in their backyards!

The point by now is clear. Give your pastor freedom to invest his money the way he wants to. Trust his wisdom and stewardship abilities. Give him at least as much freedom as you would give yourself. The Bible says to weep with those who weep and rejoice with those who rejoice. Rejoice with your pastor as he enjoys life with you! Besides, he just may invite you to his house to swim in his pool!

──STEPS TOWARD ACTION──

1. Make Jesus not only Savior, but Lord of your life.
2. Remember, you can't outgive God. Try it!
3. Practice being a generous Christian.
4. Make a commitment to tithe to your church.
5. Give from a cheerful heart.
6. Make a list of all the things God has given you and thank Him for them.
7. Follow the 10–10–80 Plan.
8. Invest your financial resources where you will have the greatest eternal impact.
9. Be supportive of a generous financial package for your pastor.
10. Give your pastor freedom to use his financial resources as he chooses.

FOR EAGLES ONLY

"When I was first asked to serve on the church board, I wondered what I could possibly do to help the pastor with the spiritual matters of the church," said Dick Peterson. "After all, he was the spiritual one called by God, not me. I had no idea of the blessing that was to come."

Here is Dick's story:

My pastor mentored those of us on the church board. We met once a month on a Saturday morning, ate breakfast, and studied spiritual leadership. At first, it was totally foreign to me. I had never heard about spiritual leadership in my limited amount of Bible study, but my pastor believed in me and encouraged me to develop my natural gifts. I was totally unaware that God had anything to say about higher standards for Christian leaders, and I was certainly of the opinion that spiritual leadership was the role held only by the pastor.

We began a study in Timothy and God began to speak to my heart. I quickly learned the importance of the shared role of leadership in the church. Servanthood was a key; first, I needed to be a faithful servant of God, and second, loyal to my pastor. (My pastor didn't ask for my loyalty, my heart was drawn to give it to him.) In the corporate world I was always driven by goals and objectives, and while those skills are still valuable, God revealed a higher level of leadership through things such as hope, vision, love, and prayer. This awareness, along with an intense year of Bible study and prayer, resulted in a deeper walk with God that changed my life. It was during this year that I realized I loved God more than anything else.

I discovered that one of my greatest joys in life was praying for and supporting my pastor. As a leader I consider it my responsibility to make sure my pastor receives adequate resources in terms of salary, seminars, and education, as well as time off for his family. It is my responsibility to stay in open communication with my pastor, and this means constructive feedback instead of criticism, solutions instead of problems, and being a visionary rather than a historian. Today, nothing is more exciting than to pass on the mentoring I have received and watch the next group of leaders rise up.

Dick Peterson is the president of INJOY, a ministry dedicated to developing leaders and church growth. He is married to Debbie, a wonderful wife and the mother of their three boys. Both Dick and Debbie are faithful leaders and servants of God who generously give of their time and talent to the church.

LEADER TO LEADER

This section is designed specifically for leaders because of the special relationship that exists between them. If you are a leader, wild horses couldn't stop you from reading this chapter. If you are not sure of your leadership, I encourage you to explore your leadership potential by reading through the ideas in this chapter.

There is a special chemistry that exists between leaders. The greater the leaders, the greater the chemistry. The first time I saw or experienced this unique connection I was too young in my own leadership development to contribute much spark myself, but I was perceptive enough to know it when I saw it.

It was years ago, and I was in a small private jet traveling from Marion, Indiana, to Indianapolis. There were six of us: the pilot, John Maxwell, Stuart Briscoe, Bruce Wilkinson, Lane Adams, and me. (I think I was the "leadership water boy"—I don't really know how I ended up as part of the flight manifest, but I was thrilled.) The conversation was electric. A constant stream of synergized ideas flowed from them. This was a group of leaders who, following their natural instincts, set about sharpening and being sharpened. They were men who would rather think than relax. They would rather dream about the future than critique the past, and when the jet touched down they all had grown stronger simply by being together. That was one of my first lessons in leadership. Leaders create synergy and energy, and they fuel each other to higher levels.

Here's another story of a similar nature, but with a different flavor. I was privileged to sit for part of a conversation between Dr. Orval Butcher, the founding pastor of Skyline Wesleyan Church, and Dr. Maxwell. These two men provided leadership for one church for forty-one years. There was a quiet confidence as they discussed the future of Skyline together. I could sense both men had spent much time with God about the same thing, and now the two of them were together in complete appreciation of what no one else could fully understand. The insight I received: Leaders understand each other.

These two stories are not meant to paint a picture of leadership as an elite club for only the chosen few. To the contrary, I believe leadership can be learned and developed. It does mean, however, that leaders are distinct and stand out from the crowd. This chapter is about leaders relating to leaders, and in particular, leaders relating to their pastors.

ACT WITH COURAGE AND INTEGRITY

Solid character is the foundation of leadership. Courage and integrity are at the core of character. They are the first two building blocks all leaders must possess. Courage without integrity produces a brave crook. Integrity without courage produces a cowardly saint. Neither person qualifies for leadership.

On Courage

Courage is not a commonly possessed trait, but everyone migrates toward a courageous leader. Courage doesn't always include the kind of bravery that faces a bullet, as in war or perhaps police work. Courage in the church, for example, takes on a different complexion and yet requires no less fortitude on the part of the leader. The following are three examples of courage in the church:

Stand up for what you speak up about.

General Douglas MacArthur said: "Last, but by no means least, courage—moral courage, the courage of one's convictions, the courage to see things through. The world is in a constant conspiracy against the brave. It's the age-old struggle—the roar of the crowd on one side and the voice of your conscience on the other." Followers will speak up, but leaders stand up. It's easy in the safety of your friends and supporters to speak your mind, even to do so boldly. Courage comes when you must say those same words to those who disagree. That's when you find the lump in your throat that only courage will push down.

A meeting was called in a church concerning a sensitive issue about the relational skills (or lack thereof) of a music staff member. Four or five leaders in the church who had been verbally stirring up quite a storm were all brought in one at a time to confront the issue with the person they were criticizing in the room. A cat sure got their tongues! Not one person would stand up and own his or her criticism—not very leader-like. These people were in fact influencers in the church, and not only did they forfeit some influence in that moment, their credibility as true leaders decreased in the eyes of those who knew what they said.

In another church, the annual business meeting was only a couple of weeks away. (Something every well-adjusted

Christian lives for. . . . Seriously, you can tell the relative unity, harmony, and overall success of a church by how many people attend the annual business meeting. If it's near empty, that's a good sign. It's not an indication that people don't care, but rather that everything is going well and they know it. They have more productive things to do with their time. If, on the other hand, the building is packed, watch out, because some issue is about to explode and the people have come out to watch!)

The issue of relocation was on the agenda, and two leaders were to make brief and positive comments on the project. These men were chosen because they were relocation team members who knew more details about the project than any-one else. Some of the items related to the relocation were sensitive ones, as is anything in the church when large amounts of money are involved. The time came for each man to speak for the project, taking tough questions without flinching and never wavering for a moment. Unlike the gossiping leaders I described previously, these men accepted their authority and managed it with courage.

Sacrifice your own comfort when necessary.

Winston Churchill said: "This is no time for ease and comfort. It is time to dare and endure." There are times when a leader is called upon to set the pace by stepping out of his or her comfort zone in a way that may result in personal sacrifice.

Let's return to the church relocation example. Leaders who step out in front are often called upon to declare their intentions publicly. Followers do not have such weighty requirements. In the case of relocation financial pledges, it may or may not include actually declaring the dollar amount, but the public accountability is the same. It takes not only courage to declare, but courage to move from your financial comfort zone. The sacrifice is real and tangible. For some, it meant driving the old car a few more years, for others it meant no vacation, and for still others it meant a reduced personal nest egg. To give up something, to give up anything, requires courage.

Leaders must be willing to sacrifice their popularity. I taught a large Sunday school class for about ten years. Joint Venture was a wonderful class filled with the best people I have ever known. The class had grown to approximately 250, but then began to level off and even decline a little. Skyline's second campus (Skyline East) was going strong but did not have a vibrant Sunday school program. The idea was to raise up a qualified couple to lead and teach the original class on the West Campus, while I led a team from Joint Venture out to the East Campus to pioneer Joint Venture East. Great strategy, but I never anticipated the degree of emotional impact on the people. This was a strong, deeply bonded group, who had invested a decade of their lives into one another and helping to grow the church *together*. Now, this camaraderie was being threatened. The idea was not at all popular but one we knew we needed to pursue.

I recruited fifteen couples to "Go East" with me and start a new class. Don and Terese Moser took the reins of leadership for Joint Venture West. It was in Don and Terese that I saw the quality of leadership; they were willing to sacrifice their own popularity to answer God's call and do what was right. When Don and Terese stood in total support and became actively involved in the process of helping me "multiply" Joint Venture to an east and west class, some of the "heat" was directed at them (by "heat" I mean only the natural response to learning that you may be separated from those you love and care for). They never backed down and as a result both classes did very well and grew to a combined high of over three hundred. More important than attendance was the doubling of leadership and ministry opportunities, as well as the positive impact on the young East County Skyline campus. The people of Joint Venture were true winners in Christ!

Don, Terese, and other leaders understand that you can't be

worried about what others think. You must do what God calls you to do, and trust Him for the results.

Take risks.

Leaders take risks. It's a nonnegotiable part of leadership territory. Your pastor must take risks in order to lead your church in a path of growth. Your pastor needs your support as a leader to shoulder the risks with him. There is a certain portion of risk that only your pastor can carry, but there is a larger portion that you can participate in. The power in shared risk: The greater the number of leaders owning a share of the responsibility, the greater the risk that can be taken, which means more potential for God. I remember so clearly during our part of the relocation process when John Maxwell addressed the local board on the topic of shared responsibility. He spoke candidly and from his heart. John told the men that he was more than willing to be the point man and shoulder the responsibility that only he could carry, as well as any more of the load he possibly could carry. He then shared with the men that the project was too big for him alone, and he needed leaders to take the risk with him, to own the project with the fierce commitment that comes from people who are willing to stand up and be counted. The risk included financial obligations, emotional impact, and ultimately success or failure of the project itself.

A *follower* says, "I hope they make it." A *committed follower* says, "I hope we make it." A *leader* says, "I will bring hope to the people, and see to it that we make it."

God's words to His leader Joshua after Moses' death are relevant for you today: "Be strong and very courageous. Be careful to obey all the law my servant Moses gave you; do not turn from it to the right or to the left, that you may be successful wherever you go" (Josh. 1:7).

On Integrity

Integrity is more popular than courage. In fact, in leadership circles the idea is in vogue. To actually live a life of integrity, however, is far more challenging than to live a life of courage. A leader is called upon to demonstrate his courage only on occasion, and even then it's for a relatively short period of time. Integrity, however, is required twenty-four hours a day. This in no way lessens the value of courage, but increases the value of integrity.

I define *integrity* as "doing what's right even when no one is looking." In most situations that call for courage, people are watching, and this provides extra motivation. With integrity, your character stands alone under God's watchful eye.

One of the leaders at Skyline felt God's leading to move to another state to follow a wise career move. There were a couple of months or so during the transition where all the change and adjustments left him and his family without a church. It would have been very easy to take a short sabbatical from tithing and begin again once they had found their new church home. They acted, however, with full integrity and continued their tithe to Skyline until they found a new church home.

David poses two great questions in Psalm 15:1: "LORD, who may abide in Thy tent? Who may dwell on Thy holy hill?" Look at the answer in Psalm 15:2–3: "He who walks with integrity, and works righteousness, and speaks truth in his heart. He does not slander with his tongue, nor does evil to his neighbor" (NASB). I also have provided some questions for you, but for these, you must provide the answers.

AN INTEGRITY CHECKLIST FOR LEADERS

1. *Do you maintain integrity with people?* ☐ yes ☐ no
   This is best characterized by the golden rule found in Matthew 7:12: "In everything, do to others what you would have them do to you."

2. *Do you maintain integrity with your priorities?*
   ☐ yes ☐ no
   If God, family, and church are at the top of your spoken list, are they at the top of your actual list?

3. *Do you maintain integrity with your pocketbook?*
☐ yes ☐ no
Do you cheerfully and consistently tithe a full 10 percent? Are you a generous giver?

4. *Do you maintain integrity with your partner?*
☐ yes ☐ no
Are you physically, emotionally, and spiritually faithful to your spouse? Are you committed to a pure thought life and full devotion to your spouse?

5. *Do you maintain professional integrity?* ☐ yes ☐ no
Do you do more than is required, and work as unto the Lord? Do you take only what is yours? Do you help others around you succeed?

Take these words from God to heart, as He spoke them to Solomon: "As for you, if you walk before me in integrity of heart and uprightness, as David your father did, and do all I command and observe my decrees and laws, I will establish your royal throne over Israel forever, as I promised David your father when I said, 'You shall never fail to have a man on the throne of Israel'" (1 Kings 9:4–5). The challenge God gave to Solomon is no different from the one He gives to you. Spiritual leadership requires godly integrity.

FOCUS ON YOUR PASTOR'S STRENGTHS

We all have strengths and weaknesses, and in leaders both are magnified. In your vital leader-to-leader role with your pastor it is essential that you focus on and support his strengths. You are not likely to change your pastor's gift mix, nor should you try. I am a very good organizer, but if you tried to improve my skills as a worship leader you would get very frustrated and need some serious earplugs. In contrast, I worked with a pastor who was an outstanding music and worship leader, but he couldn't organize himself out of the way of an oncoming train!

Perhaps your pastor is a great preacher but weak in attending to details. Your role is to champion his preaching and buttress his weakness in detail. Your support can take on many different forms, from helping with the details yourself to approving the hiring of a conscientious person to help manage the details. The worst thing is to attempt "converting" your pastor to a skill that just isn't natural to him. I've watched churches try to change their pastor, and the ultimate result is spilled blood and a U-Haul.

Determining your pastor's strengths and weaknesses can be a bit subjective. That's why it's important to focus on only his primary strengths and primary weaknesses. Concentrate on only productive strengths and destructive weaknesses.

Your pastor may love to lay out the graphic design for your church newsletter, and even be very good at it, but that isn't a productive strength for a leader responsible for growing a church. Computer literacy is another strength that is not productive for the growth of the church (in the context of senior pastor; computer skills are very important for general leadership). Since the senior pastor's job is to grow a church, using his skills unrelated to that is not a priority. Encourage your pastor to focus on those strengths that cause church growth. You can support him by insisting that someone else take care of those other areas in which he has skill. Support him in keeping his priorities clear and fixed.

If you were to make a list of your pastor's weaknesses—which I strongly do not recommend—you might come up with a long list. There is not much fruit in this kind of criticism. Nitpicking the small stuff never does much good. Instead, it is wise to ignore all of your pastor's weaknesses unless they are destructive.

A destructive weakness is one that, left unchecked, will cause harm to the overall well-being of the church. I am acquainted with a pastor in the Midwest who has very poor people skills. He loves God and cares about people, but he's very rough when it comes to dealing with people. This can be a destructive weakness and must be dealt with. A loving leader will come alongside his pastor and help him get the necessary coaching to improve his people skills.

LOYALTY IS ESSENTIAL

While we know that our ultimate first loyalty is to God, every church leader must settle this question: "Is my loyalty first to the mission of the church, or to the pastor?" The question is difficult and opens much debate, but the answer must be, "To the pastor." Leaders in the church must first be loyal to the pastor, then to the mission, because the pastor is assumed to be loyal to the mission. If that is true, your loyalty will be transferred directly into the mission. It doesn't work the other way around. If you are loyal to church growth, the Great Commission, or evangelism and discipleship, but not to the pastor, I can guarantee that serious problems will arise.

Loyalty to the mission rather than the pastor most often occurs in churches where there is frequent turnover in the position of the senior minister. The church members feel that they have a greater ownership than the pastor because they've been there longer. The "greater ownership" is only perceived, but it *is* true that the congregation has a larger investment than the incoming pastor does As a pastor on staff at Skyline, I remember listening to a direct comment made by a member who had been there much longer than I had. She said, "I've seen pastors come and I've seen pastors go, but I stay here and get the job done." She was telling me that she was more vested in the work than I was. I could have debated that point, but it was more important to respect what she thought and understand how she felt. At that level, she was 100 percent right, she *was* more vested than I. It is at this point that a problem often arises. If the leaders in the church who feel more vested than the pastor do not support his leadership and insist on doing things their way, the church will not grow and there is a strong possibility that one more pastor will be calling U-Haul.

Loyalty to the pastor does not mean blindly following and agreeing with everything he says or does. It means that as long as the pastor is giving biblical leadership, as a leader, you are to support your pastor even if you might do things differently yourself. In the corporate world disloyalty is called insubordination, and you can be fired for it. In the military, you can be shot for it!

REPRESENT YOUR PASTOR WELL

It was my first week of ministry at Skyline and I was as green as the Kentucky hills I left after graduating from seminary. One of my first responsibilities was to meet with a disgruntled member. I thought I was ready. I planned to arrive on the scene with the wisdom of Solomon, the courage of Joshua, and the compassion of Jesus! Little did I know I was really arriving on the scene to be someone's lunch. I received an earful, and I didn't remember *any* of what I heard being in the textbooks they gave me in school. I sat in silence, and eventually it was over. None of the steam was aimed directly at me but at the staff and church in general, but nonetheless, I felt as if I was walking across a bed of hot coals.

I came back, and like a foot soldier who had taken some shrapnel, reported to General Maxwell. I related the story and the second I was done, John asked me what I said to the church member. Said? Survival was my primary focus, and escape was my secondary focus. I don't think I said anything. Now that's leadership in action! I then received from John one of the best leadership lessons I have ever learned. John said: "If you remain silent, it is the same as saying you agree." It was true; within two days I was being quoted by this lady as having agreed with absolutely everything she said.

As a leader you must speak up with a positive focus in support of your pastor. Put him in a good light. You might be thinking, *What if I don't agree with the pastor but do with the one complaining?* You may disagree with your pastor—some of your greatest value will come from your honesty with him. Expressing those thoughts, however, must be done in private between you and your pastor. A leader forfeits his right to do or say anything that will hurt the church. Undermining the pastor's leadership will definitely hurt the church. God blesses unity, not division. Express your thoughts and feelings with your pastor freely in private, but in public, support him 100 percent.

REMEMBER, YOUR PASTOR IS IN CHARGE

Bob Taylor, president of Taylor Guitars, is a down-to-earth guy, committed Christian, and wise leader. (He also builds and plays a mean guitar.) He said something in a board meeting that sparked me to write this section. We were in the sensitive time of transition at Skyline with Pastor Maxwell's resignation. The church was preparing emotionally for the coming changes. In God's providence, Bob found himself vice-chairman at that time.

He carried quite a load. He presided over the board, answered to the church, and was part of the search committee for a new pastor. At the peak of all these demands, Bob admitted insightfully, "I no more belong trying to run a church than John Maxwell and Dan Reiland belong trying to build guitars!"

Bob knows that he is a creative, entrepreneurial leader whom God gifted to build a guitar company, not a church. Bob also knows that John and I could no more build a guitar than perform brain surgery. This doesn't mean that Bob can't make a significant contribution to the leadership of the church, or that John and I couldn't sand a piece of rosewood. The significant insight of Bob's statement is his realization that neither he nor any other leader should ever attempt power plays on the pastor. Bob has always been completely supportive, but many church leaders are not. As I listen to stories pastors tell about their church leaders and particularly board members, I can tell that many of these leaders believe *they*, rather than the pastor, are in charge of the church. God did not call them to this place of authority and responsibility. If you are a leader in your church, please support your pastor's leadership—don't fight it. Remember that the authority your pastor has was given by God and your church is a heavy load of servanthood, a cross you may not want to carry. Be careful what you pick up!

RELATIONSHIP IS BASED ON MUTUAL TRUST AND RESPECT

There are two things that must always exist between leaders, and they are trust and respect. If either is missing, the leader-to-leader relationship will be weak and unstable. If you trust your pastor but don't respect him, you will not follow him. If you respect your pastor (his ability), but don't trust him, you will not be loyal.

Trust is like gravity; it holds everything together. Without gravity there is chaos. Gravity is strange; you can't see it, touch it, or smell it, but you can count on it. It's kind of like taxes, no one *really* knows how the system works, but you can rest assured taxes not only exist, they will increase. You can count on them!

Three Main Components of Trust

Risk.

Anytime you trust someone you risk the success or failure of that trust. You are personally at risk because of the hurt sustained when trust is broken.

Honesty.

Honesty is the part of your character that makes you trustworthy. It is trustworthiness that makes a trusting relationship possible.

Expectation.

Expectations are part of all relationships and if not clearly established, communicated, and met, the relationship will suffer. This is true in marriages, between business partners, and with your pastor. It is important for the primary leaders in the church to have a clear understanding with the pastor of the expectations of his ministry. Without these you are all set up for frustration, or even failure.

You don't have to be the Rodney Dangerfield of your church. You can get respect! If you respect someone you basically consider him worthy of high regard or esteem.

Three Principles to Establish Respect

1. You must be willing to earn it.

Respect isn't free and no one owes it to you; you must earn it. Respect is earned over a period of time in which your character and competence maintain high standards.

2. You must be willing to sacrifice being liked.

Being respected *and* liked is certainly the preferred choice of any leader. There are times, however, when a leader must give up being liked, at least temporarily, while he or she does the right thing. Doing what is right and in the people's best interest is far more important than popularity.

Joyce Brothers said, "Don't always try to be popular. It isn't possible for everyone to like you. It's far more important for you to like yourself. And when you respect yourself, strangely, you get more respect than if you court it from others."

3. You must be willing to give it.

Ari Kiev said: "If you wish others to respect you, you must show respect for them. For twenty days, approach everyone you meet, irrespective of his station in life, as if he or she were the most important person in the world. Everyone wants to feel he counts for something and is important to someone. Invariably, people will give their love, respect,

and attention to the person who fills that need. Considera-
tion for others generally reflects faith in self and faith in
others."

I can think of many leaders I respect, but few more than Dr.
Charles Blair, who pastors Calvary Temple in Denver, Col-
orado. During a capital stewardship drive for a major building project, there arose some complex financial difficulties
created by those responsible for managing the money. Dr.
Blair was innocent yet held responsible as the senior minister
of the church. Bankruptcy could have cleared the decks, but
instead, Dr. Blair spent the next sixteen years of his life raising and paying back the seventeen million dollars of his congregation's lost money. He has pastored this great church for
more than fifty years.

It is this kind of character that inspires others to live a life
of integrity that gains profound respect. Dr. Blair will tell you
that the herculean tasks in life are achieved by doing the little
things, the right things, one day at time.

HOW TO BE YOUR PASTOR'S FRIEND

The following five areas are in some ways a review of
many of the ideas in the book but with a focus on friendship.
Not everyone can be a close friend, or even casual friend *of*
the pastor, but everyone can be a friend *to* the pastor. This
brief outline will give you practical insights to the design of
your relationship with your pastor.

Five Ways to Befriend Your Pastor

1. Know your pastor's heart.

Look beyond the surface mechanical parts of the ministry
that must be performed, and trust his heart for the Lord. From
knowing his vision to knowing the things in life that are
important to him, you can better know his heart. Allow room
for warmth and joy to be a vital part of your relationship.

2. Let your pastor be himself.

This was addressed in depth in Chapter 2, but in review, support your pastor's humanity. Don't put unrealistic, superhuman expectations on him that you wouldn't put on yourself. Encourage your pastor to be himself, and he will be far more effective!

3. Give your pastor the gift of time.

Don't put extra demands on your pastor's time, even if, and especially if, you are close friends. John Maxwell and I enjoy a wonderful friendship, but I am very sensitive about "taking" his time. He never begrudges time with me at all, but I am aware of the demands on his schedule. One of my gifts to him is to try and do things to save him time.

4. Encourage your pastor.

Be a positive influence in the life of your pastor. Be a leader who brings solutions rather than problems to the table. Let him know you appreciate all he does.

5. Seek ways to support your pastor.

Take the initiative and find ways to creatively support your pastor. You can write short, encouraging notes that do not ask your pastor to *do* anything. You can write a note that expresses appreciation or perhaps communicates a helpful ministry idea. I have watched supportive laymen do things from washing their pastor's car to conducting research for sermon preparation. There is no end to the list. Remember that you are not only helping your pastor, you are partnering with God to help build *His* church.

STEPS TOWARD ACTION

1. Seek God's direction and your pastor's assistance for your leadership development.
2. Have the courage to stand up for the things you feel strongly about.

3. Be courageous enough to sacrifice your own comfort level and take leadership risks.
4. Be steadfast in your personal integrity so that you will always do the right thing—even when no one is looking.
5. Invest the time to evaluate your level of integrity using the Integrity Checklist for Leaders.
6. Focus on your pastor's strengths, and buttress his weaknesses.
7. Never violate your sense of loyalty with your pastor.
8. Represent your pastor well—make him look good! Always speak with a positive and supportive viewpoint. Do not remain silent.
9. Remember, God called your pastor, not you, to lead the church.
10. Always extend trust and respect to your pastor.
11. Be a friend to your pastor.

NOTES

Chapter 1

1. Anthony Campolo, *Who Switched tne Price Tags?* (Dallas: Word, 1987).
2. Fuller Church Growth Institute survey of pastors (1991).
3. Ibid.
4. Ibid.
5. Ibid.

Chapter 4

1. Josh McDowell, *The Secret of Loving* (San Bernardino, Calif.: Here's Life Publishers, 1985), 61.

Chapter 8

1. C. Peter Wagner, *Your Spiritual Gifts Can Help Your Church Grow* (Ventura, Calif.: Regal Books, 1994).

ABOUT THE AUTHOR

Dr. Dan Reiland is the vice president of Leadership and Church Development at INJOY. He served for thirteen years with John Maxwell at Skyline Wesleyan Church—seven as the church's executive pastor. Dan's passion is mentoring and teaching for personal and spiritual growth. Dan has equipped hundreds of laymen in the local church and has begun doing the same with pastors. His expertise in every aspect of church leadership and management makes Dan especially effective in his role as consultant and "coach" to pastors.

Dan is an ordained Wesleyan minister. He received his master's in divinity from Asbury Theological Seminary and his doctor of ministry from Fuller Theological Seminary.

Dan is happily married to his wife, Patti, and they reside in Atlanta, Georgia, with their two children, Mackenzie and John-Peter.